200 Questions
About the Bible
and the Qur'an

Register This New Book

Benefits of Registering*

- ✓ FREE **replacements** of lost or damaged books
- ✓ FREE **audiobook** – *Pilgrim's Progress*, audiobook edition
- ✓ FREE information about new titles and other **freebies**

www.anekopress.com/new-book-registration

*See our website for requirements and limitations.

200 Questions
About the Bible
and the Qur'an

A Comparison of the Holy Books Showing
Important Similarities and Differences

Daniel Wickwire

We love hearing from our readers. Please contact us at www.anekopress.com/questions-comments with any questions, comments, or suggestions.

Visit Daniel's website: www.danwickwire.com
200 Questions about the Bible and the Qur'an – Daniel Wickwire
Copyright © 2018
First edition published 2013
All rights reserved. No part of this book may be reproduced, stored in a retrieval system, or transmitted in any form or by any means – electronic, mechanical, photocopying, recording, or otherwise, without written permission from the publisher.

Scripture taken from the King James Version (KJV), which is in the public domain.

Cover Design: J. Martin
Cover Image: By Extezy/Shutterstock
eBook Icon: Icons Vector/Shutterstock
Editor: Sheila Wilkinson

Printed in the United States of America
Aneko Press
www.anekopress.com
Aneko Press, Life Sentence Publishing, and our logos are trademarks of
Life Sentence Publishing, Inc.
203 E. Birch Street
P.O. Box 652
Abbotsford, WI 54405

RELIGION / Islam / Theology
Paperback ISBN: 978-1-62245-522-5
eBook ISBN: 978-1-62245-523-2
10 9 8 7 6 5 4 3 2 1
Available where books are sold

Contents

The Holy Books 1

God and Allah 25

The Holy Spirit, Angels, Demons & Satan 51

Christ and Muhammad 66

Man and Sin 99

Salvation 110

Future Things 124

Practical Life Issues 133

Enemies and Warfare 162

Historical Events 180

Extra Verses 201

About the Author 214

The Holy Books

1

Is it accepted that the Word of God is eternal and unchangeable? (Lev-i Mahfuz)

^{Bible} **Yes** / **Yes** ^{Qur'an}

Matthew 5:18 – For verily I say unto you, Till heaven and earth pass, one jot or one tittle shall in no wise pass from the law.

Isaiah 40:8 – The grass withereth, the flower fadeth, but the word of our God shall stand forever.

John 1:1 – In the beginning was the Word, and the Word was with God, and the Word was God.

1 Peter 1:23 – Being born again, not of corruptible seed, but of incorruptible, by the Word of God, which liveth and abideth forever.

Yunus 10:64 – There is good news in this world and in the Hereafter. No change can there be in the words of Allah. This is the supreme triumph.

Kaf 50:29 – My word cannot be changed.

* * * *

Note: In Islamic history, there were two opposing views about this subject which Muslims had internal wars over. The Mu'tazelites said no to this question, and the Ash'arites said yes. Most Muslims today would say yes.

2

Is it accepted that the Holy Bible is the Word of God? (Tevrat, Zebur & Injil)

Bible **Yes** / **Yes** Qur'an

Romans 15:4 – For whatsoever things were written aforetime were written for our learning, that we, through patience and comfort of the scriptures, might have hope.

1 Corinthians 14:37 – If any man think himself to be a prophet, or spiritual, let him acknowledge that the things that I write unto you are the commandments of the Lord.

2 Timothy 3:16-17 – (16) All scripture is given by inspiration of God, and is profitable for doctrine, for reproof, for correction, for instruction in righteousness: (17) that the man of God may be perfect thoroughly furnished unto all good works.

2 Peter 1:20-21 – (20). the scripture... (21) came not in old time by the will of man, but holy men of God spake as they were moved by the Holy Ghost.

Al-i İmran 3:119 – and you believe in all the Scripture.

Nisa 4:136 – O you who believe! Believe in ... the Scripture which He revealed before (you).

Ankebut 29:46 – And say: "We believe in that which has been revealed unto us and revealed unto you.

Shura 42:15 – Say: "I believe in whatever Book Allah has sent ... Let there be no argument between us.

3

Did God choose to communicate the written oracles of God in the Bible specifically through the agency of the Jews?

^{Bible} **Yes** / **Yes** ^{Qur'an}

Romans 3:1-2 – (1) What advantage then hath the Jew? Or what profit is there of circumcision? (2) Much every way: chiefly because that unto them were committed the oracles of God.

Romans 11:1-2 – (1) I say, then, Hath God cast away his people? God forbid. For I also am an Israelite, of the seed of Abraham, of the tribe of Benjamin. (2) God hath not cast away his people whom he foreknew.

Romans 9:4 – The Israelites; to whom pertaineth the adoption, and the glory, and the covenants, and the giving of the law, and the service of God, and the promises.

Ankebut 29:27 – We bestowed on him Isaac and Jacob, and We established the Prophethood and the Scripture among his seed.

Jathiyah 45:16 – Before this, We had bestowed on the Children of Israel the Book and the Command and the Prophethood, and provided them with good things, and favored them above (all) peoples.

4

Did God give the prophets of the Bible the ability to do obvious miracles as a confirmation that they were sent by God?

^{Bible} **Yes** / **Yes** ^{Qur'an}

Exodus 10:2 – Tell in the ears of thy son ... my signs which I have done among them; that ye may know how that I am the LORD.

John 14:11 – Believe me for the very works' sake.

John 20:30-31 – (30) And many other signs truly did Jesus in the presence of his disciples, which are not written in this book; (31) But these are written, that ye might believe that Jesus is the Christ, the Son of God; and that believing ye might have life through his name.

Hebrews 2:4 – God also bearing them witness, both with signs and wonders, and with divers miracles and gifts of the Holy Ghost.

Bakara 2:92 – Moses came to you with clear signs.

Al-i İmran 3:49 – By Allah's leave I shall give sight to the blind, heal the leper, and raise the dead to life ... Surely that will be a sign for you, if you are believers.

Al-i İmran 3:183 – Say (to them, O Muhammad): "Messengers came to you before me ... who came wth miracles, and with the Psalms, and with the Scripture giving light."

5

Does God want to protect all of His Holy Books from change and corruption? (Purpose /Niyet)

^{Bible} **Yes / Yes** ^{Qur'an}

Deuteronomy 10:17 – the LORD your God is God of gods, and Lord of lords, a great God, a mighty, and a terrible...

2 Chronicles 20:6 – none is able to withstand thee.

Psalm 12:6-7 – (6) The words of the LORD are pure words ... (7) Thou shalt keep them, O LORD, thou shalt preserve them from this generation forever.

Isaiah 14:24, 26-27 – (24) The LORD of hosts hath sworn, saying, Surely as I have thought, so shall it come to pass; and as I have purposed, so shall it stand ... (26) This is the purpose that is purposed upon the whole earth ... (27) For the LORD of hosts hath purposed, and who shall disannul it? And his hand is stretched out, and who shall turn it back?

Matthew 24:35 – Heaven and earth shall pass away, but my words shall not pass away.

Yunus 10:64 – No change can there be in the words of Allah. This is the supreme triumph.

Hijr 15:9 – We have, without doubt, sent down the Reminder, and we Preserve it.

Saffat 37:3, 7 – (3) Read (the word) for a reminder ... (7) We protect it with security from every froward devil.

6

Is God able to protect all of His Holy Books from change and corruption? (Power / Kudret)

^{Bible} **Yes / Yes** ^{Qur'an}

Deuteronomy 10:17 – the LORD your God is God of gods, and Lord of lords, a great God, a mighty, and a terrible...

2 Chronicles 20:6 – none is able to withstand thee.

Isaiah 46:9-10 – (9) For I am God ... (10) My counsel shall stand, and I will do all my pleasure.

Mark 12:24 – Do ye not therefore err, because ye know not the scriptures, neither the power of God?

Luke 21:33 – Heaven and earth shall pass away: but my words shall not pass away.

John 10:35 – The scripture cannot be broken.

En'am 6:34 – There is none to alter the decisions of Allah.

En'am 6:115 – There is nothing that can change His words.

Yunus 10:64 – No change can there be in the words of Allah. This is the supreme triumph.

Jinn 72:26-28 – (27) To every messenger whom He has chosen, and then He sends down guardians who walk before him and behind him. (28) That He may know that they have indeed conveyed the message.

7

Would God ever allow Satan, demons or mankind to thwart His own purpose and power by changing and corrupting the actual text of the Holy Books which He sent? (Tahrif bi'l-lafz)

^{Bible} **No** / **No** ^{Qur'an}

Isaiah 55:11 – So shall my word be that goeth forth out of my mouth: it shall not return unto me void, but it shall accomplish that which I please, and it shall prosper in the thing whereto I send it.

Mark 12:24 – Do ye not therefore err, because ye know not the scriptures, neither the power of God?

Luke 16:17 – It is easier for heaven and earth to pass, than one tittle of the law to fail.

Hajj 22:52 – We never sent a messenger or prophet before you, but ... Satan cast into his desire some affair. But Allah abrogates what Satan casts. Then Allah establishes (perfects) His signs (revelations) ... Allah is All Knowing.

Saffat 37:3, 7 – (3) Read (the word) ... (7) We protect it with security from every froward devil.

Hakka 69:44-47, 51 – (44) And if he had invented false sayings concerning Us, (45) We assuredly had taken him by the right hand and then severed his life-artery, and not one of you could have held Us off from him ... (51) It is the absolute truth.

8

Would it be possible for men to verbally distort the Holy Books by misquoting them or by interpreting them wrongly? (Tahrif bi'l-ma'na)

^{Bible} **Yes** / **Yes** ^{Qur'an}

Galatians 1:6-8 – (6) I marvel that ye are so soon removed from him that called you into the grace of Christ unto another gospel: (7) Which is not another; but there be some that trouble you, and would pervert the gospel of Christ. (8) But though we, or an angel from heaven, preach any other gospel unto you than that which we have preached unto you, let him be accursed.

Titus 1:10-11 – (10) For there are many unruly and vain talkers and deceivers, specially they of the circumcision: (11) Whose mouths must be stopped, who subvert whole houses, teaching things which they ought not, for filthy lucre's sake.

Ali-İmran 3:78 – And there is a party of them who distort the Scriptures with their tongues, that you may think that what they say is from the Scripture, when it is not from the Scripture. And they say: "It is from Allah," when it is not from Allah, and they speak a lie concerning Allah knowingly.

Mâide 5:41 – O Messenger! Do not be grieved by those who… say with their mouths: "We believe," but… their hearts believe not, and of the Jews: listeners for the sake of falsehood… changing words from their context and saying…

9

Are people who claim that the Bible has been changed or corrupted actually guilty of blaspheming the character and nature attributes of God by implying that (1) God didn't know, (2) God didn't care, or (3) God couldn't do anything about the Bible being changed? (El-Alim, Er-Rahman, Er-Rahim, El-Kadir)

^{Bible} <u>Yes</u> / <u>Yes</u> ^{Qur'an}

Psalm 94:8-9 – (8) Understand, ye brutish among the people: and ye fools, when will ye be wise? (9) He that planted the ear, shall he not hear? He that formed the eye, shall he not see?

Isaiah 14:24, 27 – (24) As I have purposed, so shall it stand. (27) For the LORD of hosts hath purposed, and who shall disannul it?

Hebrews 4:12-13 – For the Word of God is quick and powerful.

Baqara 2:20, 255 – (20) Allah has power over all things. (255) Allah! there is no god but Him, the Living, the Eternal. Neither slumber nor sleep overtakes Him ... His Throne embraces the Heavens and the earth, and it tires Him not to uphold them both.

Nisa 4:158 – Allah ... hears and sees all things.

Taha 20:5, 51-52 – (5) The Compassionate God, Who is established on the throne... (51) What then is the state of previous generations?... (52) The knowledge of that is with my Lord (recorded) in a book. My Lord never errs, nor forgets.

10

Are people who claim that the Bible has been changed or corrupted actually guilty of exalting Satan above God by implying that Satan won the battle for the Bible over God-Almighty? (El-Aziz, El-Galib, El-Jebbar, El-Muktedir)

^{Bible} **Yes / Yes** ^{Qur'an}

Psalm 94:7-9 – (7) Yet they say, The LORD shall not see, neither shall the God of Jacob regard it. (8) Understand, ye brutish among the people: and ye fools, when will ye be wise? (9) He that planted the ear, shall he not hear? He that formed the eye, shall he not see?

Hebrews 4:12-13 – (12) For the Word of God is quick and powerful ... (13) Neither is there any creature that is not manifest in his sight.

Yunus 10:21 – Some plot against Our revelations ... Surely our angels are recording your intrigues.

Hijr 15:9 – We have, without doubt, sent down the Reminder, and We preserve it.

Taha 20:5, 51-52 – (5) The Compassionate God, Who is established on the throne ... (51) What then is the state of previous generations? ... (52) The knowledge of that is with my Lord (recorded) in a book. My Lord never errs, nor forgets.

11

Would God have a double standard for His Holy Books to protect some of them but not all of them? (El-Adl, El-Hadi, El-Mumim, El-Muksit)

Bible **No** / **No** Qur'an

Psalm 12:6-7 – (6) The words of the Lord are pure words, as silver tried in a furnace of earth, purified seven times. (7) Thou shalt keep them, O Lord, thou shalt preserve them from this generation forever.

Psalm 111:7-9 – (7) The works of his hands are verity and judgment; all his commandments are sure. (8) They stand fast for ever and ever, and are done in truth and uprightness. (9) ...he hath commanded his covenant for ever...

Psalm 119:160 – Thy word is true from the beginning: and every one of thy righteous judgments endureth forever.

Luke 21:33 – Heaven and earth shall pass away: but my words shall not pass away.

Tevbe 9:111 – That is a promise binding upon Allah in the Torah and the Gospel and the Qur'an. Who is more faithful to his promise than Allah?

Hud 11:57 – My Lord is Guardian over all things.

İbrahim 14:47 – Never think that Allah will fail in his promise to his messengers. Surely Allah is Mighty, Able to Requite.

Hajj 22:47 – Allah shall never fail His promise.

12

Is the Word of God the universal and unchangeable standard by which God will judge all of mankind on the day of judgment? (El-Hakem, El-Hakk, El-Hafiz, El-Hasib)

^{Bible} **Yes / Yes** ^{Qur'an}

John 12:48 – He that rejecteth me, and receiveth not my words, hath one that judgeth him: the word that I have spoken, the same shall judge him in the last day.

Romans 3:4 – (4) God forbid: yea, let God be true, but every man a liar; as it is written, That thou mightest be justified in thy sayings, and mightest overcome when thou art judged.

Revelation 20:12 – And I saw the dead, small and great, stand before God; and the books were opened: and another book was opened, which is the book of life: and the dead were judged out of those things which were written in the books, according to their works.

Hijr 15:9-10 – (9) We have, without doubt, sent down the Reminder, and we preserve it. (10) We sent forth messengers before you, to the older nations.

Zumar 39:69-70 – (69) The book will be placed open, and the Prophets and the witnesses will be brought, and the people will be judged with full equity, and none will be wronged. (70) And each soul will be paid for whatever it had done.

13

Are believers allowed to believe in one part of the Scripture while disbelieving in another part of Scripture?

^{Bible} **No / No** ^{Qur'an}

Joshua 1:8 – This book of the law shall not depart out of thy mouth, but thou shalt meditate therein day and night...

Acts 20:27 – For I have not shunned to declare unto you the whole counsel of God.

1 Timothy 4:13, 15 – (13) ...give attendance to reading, to exhortation, to doctrine. (15) Meditate upon these things; give thyself wholly to them, that thy profiting may appear to all.

2 Timothy 3:16 – All scripture is given by inspiration of God, and is profitable for doctrine, for reproof, for correction, for instruction in righteousness.

Bakara 2:85 – Do you believe in one part of the Scripture and disbelieve in another?

Bakara 2:136, 285 – (136) Say: "We believe in ... that which was revealed to ... Moses and Jesus and the (other) prophets by their Lord. (285) We make no distinction between any of them ... believe in Allah ... His Scriptures and His messengers.

Al-i İmran 3:84, 119 – (84) We make no distinction between any of them. (119) You believe in all the scripture.

14

Does God want believers today to read and obey all of the Holy Books which He has sent?

^{Bible} **Yes / Yes** ^{Qur'an}

1 Timothy 4:15-16 – (15) Meditate upon these things; give thyself wholly to them; that thy profiting may appear to all. (16) Take heed unto thyself and unto the doctrine; continue in them: for in doing this thou shalt both save thyself and them that hear thee.

2 Timothy 2:15 – Study to shew thyself approved unto God, a workman that needeth not to be ashamed, rightly dividing the word of truth.

1 John 2:24 – Let that therefore abide in you, which you have heard from the beginning.

Al-i Imran 3:79 – Be worshippers of Allah by virtue of your constant study and teaching of the Scripture.

* * * *

Note: A word and letter count of the Holy Books which Muslims are required to believe in, reveals that the Tevrat, Zebur and Ijil make up 90% and the Qur'an only makes up 10%.

Bible: Words = 783,137 Letters 3,566,480

Qur'an: Words = 77,934 Letters 326,048

15

Is obedience to the Word of God the primary condition for a person to receive blessing in their life?

Bible **Yes / Yes** Qur'an

Deuteronomy 11:26-27 – (26) Behold, I set before you this day a blessing and a curse; (27) A blessing, if ye obey the commandments.

Deuteronomy 28:1, 13 – (1) ...if thou shalt hearken diligently unto the voice of the LORD thy God, to observe and to do all his commandments which I command thee this day, that the LORD thy God will set thee on high above all nations of the earth... (13) And the LORD shall make thee the head, and not the tail; and thou shalt be above only, and thou shalt not be beneath; if that thou hearken unto the commandments of the LORD thy God, which I command thee this day, to observe and to do them.

Deuteronomy 30:19 – I have set before you life and death, blessing and cursing; therefore choose life.

Bakara 2:2-5 – (2) This is the Book in which there is no doubt, in it is guidance for those who fear God ... (3) And who believe in ... (4) that which was sent down before you (the Books and the Prophets), and have certain faith in the Hereafter. (5) These are the people of true guidance from their Lord, and such are the successful.

16

Are people who refuse to read and obey the Bible actually under the curse of being a non-believer? (Kâfir)

^{Bible} **<u>Yes</u> / <u>Yes</u>** ^{Qur'an}

Numbers 15:31 – Because he hath despised the word of the LORD... that soul shall be utterly cut off...

Deuteronomy 28:15 – ...if thou wilt not hearken unto the voice of the LORD thy God, to observe to do all his commandments... all these curses shall come upon thee, and overtake thee.

Isaiah 5:11-14 – (11) Woe unto them that... regard not the work of the LORD... (13) because they have no knowledge... (14) Therefore hell hath enlarged herself...

Jeremiah 11:3 – Cursed be the man that obeyeth not the words of this covenant.

Hebrews 12:25-29 – (25) See that ye refuse not him that speaketh. (29) For our God is a consuming fire.

A'raf 7:36, 40-49 – (36) But they who deny Our revelations and scorn them; such are rightful owners of the Fire; they will dwell therein forever. (40) Those who deny our revelations and scorn them, for them the gates of Heaven will not be opened ... (41) Theirs will be a bed of Hell.

Ankebut 29:46-47 – (46) Argue not with the People of the Book ... (47) None deny our revelations save the disbelievers.

17

Is it accepted that the canon of Scripture was closed with the end of the book of Revelation?

^{Bible} **Yes** / **No** ^{Qur'an}

Revelation 22:18-19 – (18) For I testify unto every man that heareth the words of the prophecy of this book, If any man shall add unto these things, God shall add unto him the plagues that are written in this book; (19) And if any man shall take away from the words of the book of this prophecy, God shall take away his part out of the book of life, and out of the holy city, and from the things which are written in this book.

Al-i İmran 3:19-20 – (19) The true religion in the sight of Allah is Islam. Those who formerly received the Scripture disagreed among themselves through jealousy only after knowledge came to them ... (20) If they become Muslims they shall be rightly guided.

Tevbe 9:33 – It is He who has sent His messenger with the guidance and the religion of truth to make it triumphant above all religion.

Zuhruf 43:52 – And thus We have (O Muhammad) revealed a Spirit to you by Our Command. You did not know what was the Scripture, nor what the Faith was, but We have made it a light whereby We guide whom We will of our bondsmen. You are indeed guiding to a Right Way.

18

In order for the Qur'an to be considered as the Word of God, would it need to be in complete harmony with the historical Scripture as it was previously recorded in the Bible?

^{Bible} **Yes / No** ^{Qur'an}

Isaiah 8:20 – To the law and to the testimony: if they speak not according to this word, it is because there is no light in them.

1 Corinthians 14:32-33 – (32) And the spirits of the prophets are subject to the prophets. (33) For God is not the author of confusion but of peace, as in all churches of the saints.

Galatians 1:8 – But though we, or an angel from heaven, preach any other gospel unto you than that which we have preached unto you, let him be accursed.

2 John 1:9 – Whosoever transgresseth, and abideth not in the doctrine of Christ, hath not God. He that abideth in the doctrine of Christ, he hath both the Father and the Son.

Al-i İmran 3:85 – He who seeks a religion other than Islam, it will not be accepted from him, and he will be a loser in the Hereafter.

Ahzab 33:40 – Muhammad is not the father of any man among you, but he is the messenger of Allah and the Seal of the Prophets.

19

Does the Qur'an contain fundamental doctrinal and historical discrepancies which are diametrically opposed to what is found in the Bible?

^{Bible} **Yes / No** ^{Qur'an}

Isaiah 8:20 – To the law and to the testimony: if they speak not according to this word, it is because there is no light in them.

Galatians 1:8 – But though we, or an angel from heaven, preach any other gospel unto you than that which we have preached unto you, let him be accursed.

1 John 2:22-24 – (23) Whosoever denieth the Son, the same hath not the Father ... (24) Let that therefore abide in you, which ye have heard from the beginning ... continue in the Son, and in the Father.

2 John 1:9 – Whosoever transgresseth, and abideth not in the doctrine of Christ, hath not God.

Shuara 26:196-197 – (196) And it is in the Scriptures of the men of old. (197) Is it not a sign for them that the doctors of the Children of Israel know it?

Fussilat 41:43 – O Prophet, nothing is said to you that has not already been said to the Messengers before you.

Shura 42:15 – Say: "I believe in whatever Book Allah has sent ... Let there be no argument between us.

20

Is the concept of inspiration or revelation the same in the Qur'an as it is in the Bible?

^{Bible} **No** / **Yes** ^{Qur'an}

1 Corinthians 14:32-33 – (32) And the spirits of the prophets are subject to the prophets. (33) For God is not the author of confusion but of peace...

2 Timothy 3:16 – All scripture *is* given by inspiration of God, and *is* profitable for doctrine, for reproof, for correction, for instruction in righteousness.

2 Peter 1:20-21 – (20) Knowing this first, that no prophecy of the scripture is of any private interpretation. (21) For the prophecy came not in old time by the will of man, but holy men of God spoke as they were moved by the Holy Ghost.

Nisa 4:163 – We send revelation upon you, as We sent it upon ... Jesus ... and Solomon, and...

En'am 6:19, 93 – (19) Say: "Allah is witness between you and me. And this Qur'an has been inspired in me, that I may warn with it you and whomsoever it may reach." (93) Who is guilty of more wrong than he who forges a lie against Allah or says: "I am inspired," when he is not inspired in anything.

Shu'ara 26:196-197 – (196) it is in the Scriptures of the men of old... (197) the doctors of... Israel know it.

21

Would Jews or Christians accept the Qur'an as the Word of God?

^{Bible} **No / Yes** ^{Qur'an}

Deuteronomy 18:20-22 – (20) But the prophet, which shall presume to speak a word in my name, which I have not commanded him to speak ... even that prophet shall die ... (22) If the thing follow not, nor come to pass ... thou shalt not be afraid of him.

Isaiah 8:20 – To the law and to the testimony; if they speak not according to this word, it is because there is no light in them.

1 Corinthians 14:32-33 – (32) And the spirits of the prophets are subject to the prophets. (33) For God is not the author of confusion but of peace...

Galatians 1:8 – But though we, or an angel from heaven, preach any other gospel unto you than that which we have preached unto you, let him be accursed.

Revelation 22:18 – If any man shall add unto these things, God shall add unto him the plagues that are written in this book.

Nisa 4:82 – Will they not ponder the Qur'an? If it had been from other than Allah, they would have found therein many contradictions.

Shu'ara 26:196-197 – (196) It is in the Scriptures of the men of old. (197) Is it not a sign for them that the doctors of the Children of Israel know it?

22

After God has sent a Holy Book would He ever later feel the need to annul or abrogate some of its verses? (Mensuh & Nesih)

^{Bible} **No / Yes** ^{Qur'an}

Isaiah 40:8 – The grass withereth, the flower fadeth: but the word of our God shall stand forever.

Psalm 89:34 – My covenant will I not break, nor alter the thing that is gone out of my lips.

Luke 16:17 – And it is easier for heaven and earth to pass, than one tittle of the law to fail.

John 10:35 – The word of God came, and the scripture cannot be broken.

Bakara 2:106 – If we abrogate any verse or cause it to be forgotten, We replace it by a better or a similar one. Do you not know that Allah has power over all things?

Ra'd 13:39 – Allah blots out or confirms whatever He will, and with him is the Mother of the Book.

Nahl 16:101 – When We exchange a revelation in place of another revelation - and Allah knows best what He reveals - they say: "You are an imposter."

İsra 17:86 – And if we willed, We could certainly take away that which We have revealed to you.

23

If the Qur'an came down from the "Lord of the Worlds" and was ratified by a group of demons would this be a good sign that it came from God?

^{Bible} **No / Yes** ^{Qur'an}

John 14:30 – Hereafter ... the prince of this world cometh, and hath nothing in me.

2 Corinthians 4:3-4 – (3) If our gospel be hid ... (4) In whom the god of this world hath blinded the minds of them which believe not.

Fatih 1:2 – Praise be to Allah, the Lord of the Worlds.

Yunus 10:37 – The Qur'an could not have been invented (by one) apart from Allah ... from the Lord of the Worlds.

Ahkaf 46:29-30 – (29) We brought to you a group of jinn so that they might listen to the Qur'an ... (30) It confirms what came before it, and it guides to the Truth and to a Straight Road.

Jinn 72:1-14 – (1) Say O Muhammad: 'It has been revealed to me that a company of the jinn gave ear,' and they said: We have heard a wonderful Qur'an... (11) Among us there are righteous folk and among us there are far from that. We are sects having different rules. (14) Among us there are some who have surrendered (to Allah) and there are among us some who are unjust. Now those who surrendered to Allah, such have taken the right path.

24

Would a Holy Book have a felt need to repeatedly deny that it is from Satan?

^{Bible} **No / Yes** ^{Qur'an}

Matthew 7:15-20 – (15) Beware of false prophets ... (16) Ye shall know them by their fruits.

John 8:44-49 – (44) Ye are of your father the devil, and the lusts of your father ye will do. He was a murderer from the beginning, and abode not in the truth, because there is no truth in him ... (46) Which of you convinceth me of sin?

Nahl 16:98 – When you recite the Qur'an, seek refuge in Allah from Satan the accursed.

Sebe 34:8, 46 – (8) Has he invented a lie concerning against Allah, or is there in him a madness (inspired by a demon)? Say (unto them o Muhammad) (46) "There is no madness in your comrade."

Tekvir 81:22, 25 – (22) No, your companion (the prophet) is not mad. (25) Nor is this (the Qur'an) the utterance of an accursed Satan.

* * * *

Note: Muhammad often denied he was demon possessed: Hijr 15:6-7; Muminun 23:70; Saffat 37:36; Duhin 44:14; Tur 51:50-52; Kalem 68:51.

God and Allah

25

Do Jews, Christians and Muslims all believe that there is only one true God? (Vahdet-i Vüjüd)

^{Bible} <u>Yes</u> / <u>Yes</u> ^{Qur'an}

Deuteronomy 6:4 – Hear o Israel: The Lord our God is one LORD.

Deuteronomy 32:39 – I, even I, am he and there is no god with me...

Isaiah 43:10-11 – ...I am he; before me there was no God formed, neither shall there be after me. I, even I, am the LORD; and beside me there is no saviour.

Ephesians 4:4-6 – (4) There is ... one Spirit ... (5) one Lord ... (6) One God and Father of all, who is above all.

1 Timothy 2:5-6 – For there is one God.

James 2:19 – Thou believest that there is one God.

Bakara 2:163 – Your God is One God; there is no god but him.

Nisa 4:87, 171 – (87) Allah! There is no God save him. (171) Allah is only one God.

Maide 5:73 – There is no God save One God.

Nahl 16:22, 51 – (22) Your God is one God. (51) Do not take two Gods.

Kasas 28:70 – He is Allah; there is no God save Him.

İhlas 112:1 – Say: 'He is Allah, the One!'

26

Are most of the character and nature attributes of Allah which are found in the Qur'an in agreement with the attributes of God which are found in the Bible? (Esmaül-Husna)

^{Bible} **Yes / Yes** ^{Qur'an}

Isaiah 40:28 – Hast thou not known? Hast thou not heard, that the everlasting God, the LORD, the Creator of the ends of the earth, fainteth not, neither is weary? There is no searching of his understanding.

Bakara 2:255 – Allah! There is no god but Him, the Living, the Eternal. Neither slumber nor sleep overtakes Him. His is what is in the heavens and what is in the earth. Who can intercede with him except by His permission? He knows what is before them and what lies behind them, and they can grasp only that part of His Knowledge which he will. His Throne embraces the Heavens and the earth, and it tires Him not to uphold them both. His is the High, the Tremendous.

Kahf 18:45 – Allah has power over all things.

Hashr 59:23 – He is Allah besides whom there is no other god. He is the Sovereign Lord, the Holy One, the Source of Security the keeper of Faith; the Guardian, the Mighty One, the All Powerful.

27

Are the "God" of the Bible and the "Allah" of the Qur'an one and the same entity?

^{Bible} **No / Yes** ^{Qur'an}

Exodus 3:14 – God said unto Moses, I AM THAT I AM: and he said, Thus shalt thou say unto the children of Israel, I AM hath sent me unto you.

1 John 5:20 – Jesus Christ. This is the true God, and eternal life.

2 John 1:9 – Whosoever transgresseth, and abideth not in the doctrine of Christ, hath not God. He that abideth in the doctrine of Christ, he hath both the Father and the Son.

Matthew 28:19 – Go ye therefore, and teach all nations, baptizing them in the name of the Father, and of the Son, and of the Holy Ghost.

Ankebut 29:46 – And argue not with the People of the Book... say: "We believe in that which has been revealed unto us and revealed unto you; our God and your God is One, and unto Him we surrender."

Saffat 37:126 – Allah, your Lord and Lord of your forefathers.

Shura 42:15 – say: I believe in whatever Book Allah has sent down... Allah is our Lord as well as your Lord... let there be no argument between us.

28

Is God's eternal and unchangeable name "Yahweh"?

^{Bible} **Yes / No** ^{Qur'an}

Exodus 3:15 – The LORD (YAHWEH) God (Elohim) of your fathers, the God of Abraham, the God of Isaac, and the God of Jacob, hath sent me unto you; this is my name forever, and this is my memorial unto all generations.

Isaiah 26:4 – Trust ye in the LORD for ever: for in the LORD JEHOVAH (Yah Yahweh) is everlasting strength.

John 8:23-24, 58 – (23) I am from above. Ye are of this world. I am not of this world... (24) if ye believe not that I am he, ye shall die in your sins... (58) Jesus said unto them, Verily, verily, I say unto you, Before Abraham was, I am.

A'raf 7:180 – Allah's are the most beautiful names; so call on him by them! And leave the company of those who blaspheme His names.

Isra 17:110 – Say: "Call upon Allah ... to Him belong the most beautiful names."

* * * *

Note: God's special and eternal name "Yahweh" is used 6,823 times in the Bible but is not found at all among the 99 names of God (Esmaül-Husna) in the Quran.

Cf. Taha 20:8, Rahman 55:78, Hashr 59:24.

29

Are there verses in the Holy Books about God being holy? (el-Kuddus)

^{Bible} **Yes** / **Yes** ^{Qur'an}

1 Samuel 6:20 – Who is able to stand before this holy LORD God?

Isaiah 6:3 – Holy, holy, holy, is the LORD of hosts.

Isaiah 40:25 – To whom then will ye liken me, or shall I be equal? saith the Holy One.

Isaiah 57:15 – For thus saith the high and lofty One that inhabiteth eternity, whose name is Holy.

John 17:11 – I come to thee. Holy Father.

Revelation 4:8 – Holy, holy, holy, Lord God Almighty.

Hashr 59:23 – He is Allah besides whom there is no other god. He is the Sovereign Lord, the Holy One.

Jum'a 62:1 – Whatever is in the heavens and in the earth glorifies Allah, the Sovereign Lord, the Holy One, the Mighty, the Wise.

* * * *

Note: This attribute only appears twice in the Qur'an, but is found over 450 times in the Bible.

30

Among the character and nature attributes of God, does God reveal Himself as the Father?

^{Bible} **Yes** / **No** ^{Qur'an}

Isaiah 63:16 – Doubtless thou art our father ... thou, O LORD, art our father, our redeemer.

Isaiah 64:8 – But now, O LORD, thou art our father; we are the clay, and thou our potter, and we all are the work of thy hand.

Matthew 5:45, 48 – (45) That ye may be the children of your Father, which is in heaven; (48) Your Father, which is in heaven, is perfect.

Matthew 6:9-10 – (9) After this manner therefore pray ye: Our Father which art in heaven, Hallowed be thy name. (10) Thy kingdom come, Thy will be done...

John 8:41 – We have one Father, even God.

En'am 6:101 – The Originator of the heavens and the earth! How can He have a child, when there is for Him no consort, when He created all things and is Aware of all things?

Furkan 25:2 – No son has He begotten ... No partner has He in His sovereignty!

Jinn 72:3 – And we believe that He - exalted be the glory of our Lord! - has taken neither wife nor son.

31

Is God proud and is pride a character attribute of God? (el-Mütekebbir)

Bible **No** / **Yes** Qur'an

Psalm 101:5 – Him that hath an high look and a proud heart will not I suffer.

Proverbs 6:16-17 – (16) These six things doth the LORD hate; yea seven are an abomination unto him: (17) ... a proud look.

Proverbs 21:4 – An high look, and a proud heart, and the plowing of the wicked, is sin.

Isaiah 57:15 – For thus saith the high and lofty One who inhabiteth eternity, whose name is Holy; I dwell in the high and holy place, with him also that is of a contrite and humble spirit.

1 John 2:16 – The pride of life, is not of the Father, but is of the world.

Hashr 59:23 – He is Allah besides whom there is no other god. He is the Sovereign Lord, the Holy One, the Source of Security the keeper of Faith; the Guardian, the Mighty One, the All Powerful, the Proud!

32

Among the character and nature attributes of God, does God reveal Himself as the Savior?

^{Bible} **Yes** / <u>**No**</u> ^{Qur'an}

Isaiah 43:3, 11 – (3) For I am the LORD thy God, the Holy One of Israel, thy Saviour. (11) I, even I, am the LORD, and beside me there is no saviour.

Hosea 13:4 – I am the LORD thy God ... for there is no Saviour beside me.

Luke 2:11 – For unto you is born this day in the city of David a Saviour, which is Christ the Lord.

John 3:17 – For God sent not his Son into the world to condemn the world; but that the world through him might be saved.

Titus 1:4 – Grace, mercy, and peace, from God the Father and the Lord Jesus Christ our Saviour.

Titus 2:10-13 – (10) God our Saviour in all things. (13) great God and our Saviour Jesus Christ.

Titus 3:4-6 – (4) God our Saviour ... (6) which he shed on us abundantly through Jesus Christ our Saviour.

Jude 1:25 – To the only wise God our Saviour.

* * * *

Note: The attribute of God being a "Savior" is not found at all among the 99 names of God mentioned in the Qur'an (Esmaül-Hüsna), but is found 39 times for God in the Bible.

33

In the Holy Books when God refers to Himself, does He ever speak in the first person plural "We"?

^{Bible} **Yes** / **Yes** ^{Qur'an}

Genesis 1:26 – And God said, Let us make man in our image, after our likeness.

Genesis 3:22 – And the LORD God said, Behold, the man is become as one of us, to know good and evil...

Genesis 11:6-7 – (6) The LORD said ... (7) let us go down, and there confound their language.

Isaiah 6:8 – Also I heard the voice of the Lord, saying, Whom shall I send, and who will go for us? Then said I, Here I am; send me.

John 17:11 – And now ... I come to thee. Holy Father, keep through thine own name those whom thou hast given me, that they may be one, as we are.

Enbiya 21:91 – And (remember that blessed woman) who guarded her chastity. Then We breathed into her of Our spirit, and We made her and her son a sign for all peoples.

Vakia 56:57-59, 64, 69, 72 – (57) We created you: will you not believe? (58) Behold (the semen) you emit: (59) Do you create it or are We the Creator?

İnsan 76:23 – We, even We, have revealed to you the Qur'an by stages.

34

Is the concept of the Trinity acceptable?
(Father, Son & Holy Spirit)

^{Bible} **Yes** / **No** ^{Qur'an}

Genesis 1:26-27 – (26) And God said, Let us make man in our image... (27) So God created...

Genesis 11:6-7 – (6) the LORD said ... (7) let us go down, and there confound their language.

Matthew 28:18-20 – (18) Jesus came and spake ... (19) Go ye therefore, and teach all nations, baptizing them in the name of the Father, and of the Son, and the Holy Ghost.

Luke 1:35 – ...The Holy Ghost shall come upon thee, and the power of the Highest shall overshadow thee: therefore also that holy thing which shall be born of thee shall be called the Son of God.

Ephesians 4:4-6 – (4) There is ... one Spirit ... (5) One Lord ... (6) One God and Father of all, who is above all.

Al-i İmran 3:64 – We assign no partner to him.

Nisa 4:171 – The Messiah, Jesus son of Mary, was only a messenger of Allah ... say not "three." Cease! (it is) better for you! Allah is only One God. Far is it removed from His transcendent majesty that He should have a son.

Maide 5:72-73 – (72) Surely they disbelieve who say: "God is the Messiah ..." (73) Allah is the third of three.

35

Would God ever falsely accuse Jesus of doing something wrong or would Jesus ever lie to God to cover up something he did wrong?

Bible **No** / **Yes** Qur'an

John 7:18 – The same is true, and no unrighteousness is in him.

John 8:46 – Which of you convinceth me of sin? And if I say the truth, why do ye not believe me?

John 10:30 – I and my Father are one.

2 Timothy 2:13 – If we believe not, yet he abideth faithful: he cannot deny himself.

Titus 1:2 – In hope of eternal life, which God, that cannot lie, promised before the world began.

1 Peter 2:21-23 – (21) Christ ... (22) who did no sin, neither was guile found in his mouth.

1 John 3:5 – And ye know that he was manifested to take away our sins; and in him is no sin.

Ma'ida 5:116 – Allah said to Jesus: Did you say to mankind: "Take me and my mother for two gods beside Allah?" Jesus said: "Be glorified! It was not mine to say that to which I had no right. If I used to say it, then You knew it. You know what is in my mind, and I do not know what is in Your mind. Assuredly, You, only You are the Knower of things hidden."

36

Is God a distant, transcendental God who rarely ever shows His great power or leaves His fingerprints on human history?

^{Bible} **No** / **Yes** ^{Qur'an}

Exodus 13:21 – And the LORD went before them by day in a pillar of a cloud to lead them the way; and by night in a pillar of fire, to give them light; to go by day and night:

Exodus 16:9-10 – (9) And Moses spake ... unto all the congregation of the children of Israel ... (10) and behold, the glory of the LORD appeared in the cloud.

1 Samuel 12:16 – Stand and see this great thing, which the LORD will do before your eyes.

Matthew 17:5 – While he yet spake, behold, a bright cloud overshadowed them: and behold a voice out of the cloud, which said, This is my beloved Son, in whom I am well pleased; hear ye him.

En'am 6:37-38 – (37) They say: "Why has no sign been sent down upon him from his Lord?" Say: "Allah is certainly able to send down a sign. But most of them know not" ... (38) We have neglected nothing in the Book (of Our decrees).

Tevbe 9:30-31 – (30) Allah ... (31) Transcendent is He above what they associate with Him.

37

Has God ever shown Himself visibly to people on earth? (Theophany or Ru'yetullah)

^{Bible} **Yes** / **No** ^{Qur'an}

Exodus 33:11, 18-23 – (11) The LORD spake unto Moses face to face. (18) I beseech thee, shew me thy glory ... (23) Thou shalt see my back parts; but my face shall not be seen.

Numbers 12:7-8 – (7) My servant Moses ... (8) with him will I speak mouth to mouth ... and the similitude of the LORD shall he behold.

Isaiah 6:1-8 – (1) I saw also the LORD sitting upon a throne... (5) mine eyes have seen the King, the Lord...

En'am 6:103 – Vision comprehends him not.

A'raf 7:143 – Moses ... Show me (yourself) that I may gaze upon you ... He said: You will not see Me.

Hajj 22:63 – Surely Allah is Subtle (Latif), All-Aware.

Lokman 31:16 – Truly, Allah is Subtle (Latif), Aware.

* * * *

Note: Other Theophanies in the Bible: Genesis 12:7-9; Genesis 18:1-33; Genesis 32:22-30; Exodus 3:2-4:17; Exodus 24:9-11; Deuteronomy 31:14-15; Job 38-42.

38

Does God ever speak directly to people today aside from His written revelation?

^{Bible} **Yes / No** ^{Qur'an}

Joel 2:28 – And it shall come to pass afterward, that I will pour out my spirit upon all flesh; and your sons and your daughters shall prophesy.

Acts 2:17 – And it shall come to pass in the last days, saith God, I will pour out of my Spirit upon all flesh: and your sons and your daughters shall prophesy, and your young men shall see visions, and your old men shall dream dreams.

1 Corinthians 14:1-4, 24-31 – (1) Follow after charity, and desire spiritual gifts, but rather that ye may prophecy ... (4) He that prophesieth edifieth the church. (24) But if all prophesy, and there come in one that believeth not, or one unlearned, he is convinced of all, he is judged of all. (25) And thus are the secrets of his heart made manifest; and so falling down on his face he will worship God, and report that God is in you of a truth. (31) For ye may all prophesy one by one, that all may learn.

Tevbe 9:31 – Transcendent is He above.

Shura 42:51 – And it is not given to any mortal that Allah should speak to him unless it be by revelation or from behind a veil, or that he sends a messenger (an angel).

39

Does the infinite God desire to have a close and loving relationship with finite man such that men are called the "Children of God"?

^{Bible} <u>**Yes**</u> / <u>**No**</u> ^{Qur'an}

Hosea 1:10 – In the place where it was said unto them, Ye are not my people, there it shall be said unto them, Ye are the sons of the living God.

Galatians 4:6 – And because ye are sons, God hath sent forth the Spirit of his Son into your hearts.

1 John 3:1-2 – (1) Behold what manner of love the Father hath bestowed upon us, that we should be called the sons of God ... (2) Beloved, now are we the sons of God.

Maide 5:18 – The Jews and the Christians say: "We are the sons of Allah, and His loved ones." Say: "Why then does He chastise you for your sins? Surely you are but mortals of His creating."

* * * *

Note: While the Qur'an denies that men can become the Sons of God, God is also said to be very near to man: cf. Enfal 8:24; Hud 11:90, 92; Kaf 50:16.

40

Is the love of God unconditional? (el-Vedud)

^{Bible} **Yes** / **No** ^{Qur'an}

John 3:16 – For God so loved the world, that he gave his only begotten Son, that whosoever believeth in him should not perish, but have everlasting life.

Romans 5:8 – But God commendeth his love toward us, in that, while we were yet sinners, Christ died for us.

1 John 4:8-10 – (8) God is love. (9) In this was manifested the love of God toward us, because that God sent his only begotten Son into the world, that we might live through him. (10) Herein is love, not that we loved God, but that he loved us, and sent his Son to be the propitiation for our sins.

Revelation 22:17 – Come... And let him that is athirst come. And whosoever will, let him take the water of life freely.

Bakara 2:195, 276 – (195) And know that Allah loves the doers of good. (276) He does not love the impious and guilty.

Al-i İmran 3:57, 159 – (57) Allah loves not the wrongdoers. (159) Allah loves those that trust in Him.

Nisa 4:107 – Allah loves not one who is ... sinful.

Rum 30:45 – Allah loves not the disbelievers.

41

Does God look on believers as being merely His slaves or servants?

^{Bible} **No** / **Yes** ^{Qur'an}

John 1:12-13 – (12) But as many as received him, to them gave he power to become the sons of God, even to them that believe on his name: (13) Which were born, not of... the will of man, but of God.

John 15:15 – Henceforth I call you not servants; for the servant knoweth not what his Lord doeth: but I have called you friends.

1 Peter 2:5, 9-10 – (5) Ye also, as lively stones, are built up a spiritual house, an holy priesthood, to offer up spiritual sacrifices, acceptable to God by Jesus Christ. (9) But ye are a chosen generation, a royal priesthood, an holy nation, a peculiar people. (10) Which in time past were not a people, but are now the people of God.

Revelation 21:1-2 – (1) And I saw a new heaven and a new earth... and... (2) a bride adorned for her husband.

Revelation 22:17 – the Spirit and the bride say, Come.

Sad 38:83 – Your single minded slaves.

Zumar 39:16 – This is the doom with which Allah frightens His bondsmen. So, O my servants, avoid my wrath.

Shura 42:19 – Allah is kind to his slaves.

42

Does God show any favoritism among people and prefer some above others?

^{Bible} **No / Yes** ^{Qur'an}

Mark 12:14 – Master, we know that thou art true, and carest for no man; for thou regardest not the person of men.

Galatians 3:28 – There is neither Jew nor Greek, there is neither bond nor free, there is neither male nor female; for ye are all one in Christ Jesus.

Ephesians 6:9 – Your Master also is in heaven; neither is there respect of persons with him.

Bakara 2:228, 282 – (228) women have rights similar to those of men… and men are a degree above them.

En'am 6:165 – He it is who has placed you as vicegerents of the earth and has exalted some of you in rank above others.

Nahl 16:71, 75 – (71) Allah has favored some of you above others. (75) Are they (at all) equal?

Ahzab 33:50 – O prophet! We have made lawful unto you your wives … A privilege for you only, not the rest of believers.

* * * *

Note: cf. Hadith: Mishkat ul-Masabih, Vol. 3, p. 117 and Bukhari Vol. 1, no. 28, 301; Vol. 2, no. 161.

43

Does God especially hate certain sinners and want to send some of them to hell?

^{Bible} **No** / **Yes** ^{Qur'an}

Ezekiel 18:23, 32 – (23) Have I any pleasure at all that the wicked should die? (32) I have no pleasure in the death of him that dieth ... wherefore turn yourselves, and live.

Jeremiah 3:22 – Return, ye backsliding children, and I will heal your backslidings.

Luke 14:23 – And the lord said... compel them to come in, that my house may be filled.

1 Timothy 2:3-4 – (3) For this is good and acceptable in the sight of God, our Saviour, (4) Who will have all men to be saved, and to come unto the knowledge of the truth.

2 Peter 3:9 – The Lord is not slack concerning his promise, as some men count slackness; but is longsuffering to us-ward, not willing that any should perish, but that all should come to repentance.

Maide 5:41 – Those are they for whom the will of Allah is that He cleanse not their hearts.

A'raf 7:179 – Already We have urged to hell many of the jinn and humankind ... These are a cattle. No, but they are worse!

Tevbe 9:55 – Allah wills to punish them ... and that their souls shall pass away while they are disbelievers.

44

Is God the author of good and evil and responsible for doing both? (Hayır & Sher)

^{Bible} **No** / **Yes** ^{Qur'an}

Jeremiah 29:11 – I know the thoughts that I think toward you ... thoughts of peace, and not of evil.

James 1:13, 17 – (13) Let no man say when he is tempted, I am tempted of God: for God cannot be tempted with evil, neither tempteth he any man... (17) Every good gift is from above, and cometh down from the Father of lights, with whom is no variableness, neither shadow of turning.

Bakara 2:26 – Allah leads astray many.

Nisa 4:78 – And if an evil befalls them, say: "All is from Allah."

Maide 5:14 – Those who say ... "we are Christians" we have stirred up enmity and hatred among them.

Enbiya 21:35 – We test you with evil and with good as a trial.

Sejde 32:13 – I will fill Hell with Jinn and mankind altogether.

Zuhruf 43:36 – we set a devil upon him.

* * * *

Note: In the Bible there are places where God allows adversity or calamity (not moral evil) to befall man: Isa. 45:7; Jer. 4:6; Amos 3:6. But Satan is seen as the author of evil: Jn. 8:44; 1 Jn. 3:8.

45

Would God be described as the greatest plotter or schemer of them all? (Makara)

_{Bible} **No / Yes** _{Qur'an}

Genesis 3:1, 13 – (1) Now the serpent was more subtle than any beast of the field... (13) And the woman said, The serpent beguiled me, and I did eat.

Habakkuk 1:13 – Thou art of purer eyes than to behold evil, and canst not look on iniquity.

Micah 2:1 – Woe to them that devise iniquity, and work evil on their beds.

Zechariah 8:17 – Let none of you imagine evil in your hearts against his neighbour, and love no false oath: for all these are things that I hate, saith the LORD.

Al-i İmran 3:54 – And they (the disbelievers) schemed, and Allah schemed (against them); and Allah is the best of schemers.

Ra'd 13:42 – All plotting is (in the hand) of Allah.

Neml 27:50 – So they plotted, and We plotted.

* * * *

Note: In the Bible plotting and scheming are seen as being evil, and these activities are attributed to Satan, not God: cf. Genesis 3:1; Esther 9:25; Psalm 21:11; Psalm 36:4; Proverbs 1:30; 2 Corinthians 11:13-15; Ephesians 6:11; 1 Peter 5:8-9; 2 John 1:7.

46

Is God responsible for casting enmity and hatred among people of different faiths?

^{Bible} **No / Yes** ^{Qur'an}

2 Timothy 2:13 – If we believe not, yet he abideth faithful; he cannot deny himself.

James 1:13 – Let no man say when he is tempted, I am tempted of God; for God cannot be tempted with evil, neither tempteth he any man.

Jeremiah 29:11 – For I know the thoughts that I think toward you, saith the Lord, thoughts of peace, and not of evil, to give you an expected end.

Habakkuk 1:13 – Thou art of purer eyes than to behold evil, and canst not look on iniquity.

Bakara 2:10 – In their hearts is a disease, so Allah has increased their disease.

Nisa 4:88 – Would you guide those whom Allah has sent astray? He whom Allah has sent astray, for him (O Muhammad) never can you find a way.

Maide 5:14 – And with those who say "Surely we are Christians" we have stirred up enmity and hatred among them.

Maide 5:64 – The Jews ... We have cast among them enmity and hatred till the Day of Resurrection.

47

Is it God's heart to harden some men's hearts and lead them astray?

Bible **No** / **Yes** Qur'an

Matthew 18:11-14 – (11) For the Son of man is come to save that which was lost. (12) If a man have an hundred sheep, and one of them be gone astray ... (14) Even so it is not the will of your Father which is in heaven, that one of these little ones should perish.

1 Timothy 2:3-4 – (3) God our Saviour, (4) Who will have all men to be saved, and to come unto the knowledge of the truth.

2 Timothy 2:26 – And that they may recover themselves out of the snare of the devil, who are taken captive by him at his will.

James 1:13 – Let no man say when he is tempted, "I am tempted of God." For God cannot be tempted with evil, neither tempteth he any man.

Baqara 2:7, 15, 26 – (7) Allah has set a seal on their hearts and on their hearing. (15) Allah (Himself) does mock at them, leaving them to wander blindly in their rebellion. (26) Allah leads astray many.

Nisa 4:119 – And surely I will lead them astray, and surely I will arouse desires in them.

A'raf 7:186 – Whomsoever Allah sends astray, none can guide him; and He lets them wander blindly.

48

Is God's character and behavior ever capricious or whimsical?

^{Bible} **No / <u>Yes</u>** ^{Qur'an}

Numbers 23:19 – Hath he said, and shall he not do it? Or hath he spoken and shall he not make it good?

Psalm 119:90 – Thy faithfulness is unto all generations.

Malachi 3:6 – For I am the LORD, I change not.

2 Timothy 2:13 – If we believe not, yet he abideth faithful; he cannot deny himself.

Titus 1:2 – God, that cannot lie, promised.

James 1:13 – ...God cannot be tempted with evil, neither tempteth he any man.

Hud 11:106-108 – (106) As for the wretched, they shall be in the Fire... (107) Eternally therein... unless your Lord ordains otherwise... For your Lord is doer of what He wills. (108) And as for the blessed, they shall dwell eternally in the Gardens... unless your Lord ordains.

Hajj 22:14 – Surely Allah does what He pleases.

Fatir 35:8 – Allah verily misleads whom he wills and guides whom He wills.

Buruj 85:16 – Doer of whatever He wills.

49

Is it forbidden to prostrate oneself before anyone other than God Himself?

^{Bible} **Yes** / **Yes** ^{Qur'an}

Exodus 20:2-5 – (2) I am the LORD thy God ... (3) Thou shalt have no other gods before me ... (5) Thou shalt not bow down thyself to them, nor serve them; for I, the LORD thy God am a jealous God.

Exodus 34:14 – For thou shalt worship no other god; for the LORD whose name is Jealous, is a jealous God...

Deuteronomy 5:7-9 – (7) Thou shalt have none other gods before me ... (9) Thou shalt not bow down thyself unto them ... for I the LORD thy God am a jealous God.

Matthew 4:10 – Thou shalt worship the Lord, thy God, and him only shalt thou serve.

Revelation 22:8-9 – (8) I fell down to worship before the feet of the angel ... (9) Saith he unto me, See thou do it not; for I am thy fellow servant, and of thy brethren the prophets, and of them which keep the sayings of this book: Worship God.

İsra 17:23 – Your Lord has decreed that you worship none but Him.

Zariyat 51:56 – I created jinn and humankind only that they might worship me.

50

Did God issue a command contrary to His own eternal law ordering all of the angels to "Prostrate yourselves before Adam"?

Bible <u>No</u> / <u>Yes</u> Qur'an

Isaiah 14:12-14 – (12) How art thou fallen from heaven, O Lucifer ... (13) For thou hast said in thine heart ... I will exalt my throne above the stars of God ... (14) I will be like the most High.

Ezekiel 28:11-19 – (15) Thou wast perfect ... till iniquity was found in thee. (17) Thine heart was lifted up because of thy beauty; thou hast corrupted thy wisdom by reason of thy brightness.

Bakara 2:31-34 – (34) And when we said to the angels: "Prostrate yourselves before Adam!" they all prostrated themselves, except Satan.

A'raf 7:11-18 – (11) Then told the angels; "Fall prostrate before Adam!" and they fell prostrate.

İsra 17:61-65 – (61) When we said ... "Prostrate yourselves before Adam!" they all prostrated themselves except Iblis, who said: "Shall I bow to him whom you have made of clay?"

Kehf 18:50-51 – (50) We said to the angels; "Prostrate yourselves before Adam!" all prostrated themselves, except Satan.

Sad 38:71-78 – (72) When I have fashioned him and breathed into him of my spirit, then fall down before him prostrate... (73) the angels fell down...(74) except Iblis.

The Holy Spirit, Angels, Demons & Satan

51

Is the Holy Spirit accepted as God? (Ruh-ül Kudüs)

^{Bible} **Yes / No** ^{Qur'an}

Genesis 1:1-2 – (1) In the beginning God created the heaven and the earth... (2) And the Spirit of God moved upon the face of the waters.

Psalm 139:7 – Whither shall I go from thy spirit? Or whither shall I flee from thy presence?

John 4:24 – God is a Spirit; and they that worship him must worship him in spirit and in truth.

Acts 5:3-4 – (3) Why hath Satan filled thine heart to lie to the Holy Ghost ... (4) Thou hast not lied unto men, but unto God.

Bakara 2:87, 253 – (87) We gave Jesus son of Mary the clear miracles and strengthened him with the Holy Spirit (the Angel Gabriel).

Maide 5:110 – O Jesus, son of Mary ... I strengthened you with the holy spirit (the archangel Gabriel).

* * * *

Note: There are 113 places in the Bible where the Holy Spirit is depicted as being God.

52

Does the Holy Spirit have the power to create?

^{Bible} **Yes / No** ^{Qur'an}

Genesis 1:1-2 – (1) In the beginning God created the heaven and the earth. (2) And the Spirit of God moved upon the face of the waters.

Job 26:13 – By his spirit he hath garnished the heavens.

Job 33:4 – The Spirit of God hath made me, and the breath of the Almighty hath given me life.

Psalm 104:30 – Thou sendest forth thy spirit, they were created.

Hebrews 9:14 – through the eternal spirit...

Maide 5:110, 116, 118 – (110) O Jesus, son of Mary ... I strengthened you with the holy spirit (the archangel Gabriel). (116) Assuredly, You, only You are the Knower of things hidden. (118) You, only You, are the Mighty, the Wise.

Meryem 19:17-19 – We sent to her Our spirit (Gabriel) ... He said: "I am only a messenger of your Lord."

✶ ✶ ✶ ✶

Note: In Many translations of the Quran, where the words Holy Spirit are found, the translators put the word (Gabriel) in parenthesis to equate the Holy Spirit with the angel Gabriel.

53

Are the Holy Spirit and the angel Gabriel one and the same?

Bible **No** / **Yes** Qur'an

Luke 1:11-35 – (11) There appeared unto him an angel of the Lord ... (13) The angel said ... Zacharias ... thy wife Elisabeth shall bear thee a son, and thou shalt call his name John. (15) He shall be filled with the Holy Ghost, even from his mother's womb. (19) And the angel ... said unto him, I am Gabriel, that stand in the presence of God, and am sent to speak unto thee, and to shew thee these glad tidings.

John 4:24 – God is a Spirit.

Bakara 2:87, 98 – (87) We gave Jesus son of Mary the clear miracles (to serve as proofs of Allah's sovereignty) and strengthened him with the Holy Spirit (the angel Gabriel) ... Say (O Muhammad, to them). (98) Who is an enemy to Allah, and His Angels and His Messengers, and to Gabriel and Michael?

* * * *

Note: Within Islam the Holy Spirit is generally depicted as being the angel Gabriel.

54

Is blasphemy against the "Holy Spirit" the one and only unpardonable sin?

^{Bible} **<u>Yes</u> / <u>No</u>** ^{Qur'an}

Matthew 12:31-32 – (31) All manner of sin and blasphemy shall be forgiven men; but the blasphemy against the Holy Ghost shall not be forgiven unto men. (32) And whosoever speaketh a word against the Son of man, it shall be forgiven him; but whosoever speaketh against the Holy Ghost, it shall not be forgiven him, neither in this world, neither in the world to come.

Mark 3:29 – But he that shall blaspheme against the Holy Ghost, hath never forgiveness, but is in danger of eternal damnation.

1 John 5:16 – There is a sin unto death…

Nisa 4:48, 116, 168 – (48) Allah will not forgive those who assign partners to him. (116) Allah forgives not that partners should be ascribed to him. Whoever ascribes partners to Allah has strayed far indeed. (168) Those who reject faith and do wrong, Allah will never forgive them, neither will He guide them to a road.

Tevbe 9:80 – Whether you ask forgiveness for them or not (their sin is unforgivable); if you ask forgiveness for them seventy times, Allah will not forgive them. That is because they have denied Allah and his messenger…

55

Are the Holy Books focused upon the things of the Spirit?

^{Bible} **Yes / No** ^{Qur'an}

Ephesians 6:12, 18 – (12) For we wrestle not against flesh and blood, but against... spiritual wickedness in high places... (18) Praying always with all prayer and supplication in the Spirit...

Romans 1:11 – For I long to see you, that I may impart unto you some spiritual gift, to the end ye may be established.

Romans 8:9 – But ye are not in the flesh but in the Spirit, if so be that the Spirit of God dwell in you. Now if any man have not the Spirit of Christ, he is none of his.

1 Corinthians 2:13-16 – (13) Things also we speak ... in the words ... which the Holy Ghost teacheth, comparing spiritual things with spiritual ... (15) But he that is spiritual judgeth all things.

1 Peter 2:5 – Ye also, as living stones, are built up a spiritual house, an holy priesthood to offer up spiritual sacrifices, acceptable to God...

Jude 18-19 – (18) They told you there should be mockers in the last time, who should walk after their own ungodly lusts. (19) These be they who separate themselves, sensual, having not the Spirit.

İsra 17:85 – They ask you about the Spirit. Say: "The Spirit is of my Lord's command, and of knowledge you have been given but little."

56

Does God's Holy Spirit indwell believers and empower them with spiritual gifts?

^{Bible} **Yes / No** ^{Qur'an}

John 20:21-22 – (21) Then said Jesus ... as my Father hath sent me, even so send I you. (22) ... He breathed on them, and saith unto them, Receive ye the Holy Ghost.

Acts 1:8 – But ye shall receive power, after that the Holy Ghost is come upon you.

Romans 8:9 – But ye are not in the flesh but in the Spirit, if so be that the Spirit of God dwell in you. Now if any man have not the Spirit of Christ, he is none of his.

1 Corinthians 12:1, 4-11, 13 – (1) Now concerning spiritual gifts, brethren, I would not have you ignorant ... (7) The manifestation of the Spirit is given to every man to profit. (13) For by one Spirit are we all baptized into one body, whether we be Jew or Gentiles, whether we be bond or free; and have been all made to drink into one Spirit.

* * * *

Note: The Qur'an does not mention spiritual gifts nor the indwelling of the Holy Spirit.

57

Can spiritual gifts be imparted from one believer to another by the laying on of hands?

Bible <u>Yes</u> / <u>No</u> Qur'an

Romans 1:11 – For I long to see you, that I may impart unto you some spiritual gift, to the end that ye may be established.

1 Timothy 4:14-15 – (14) Neglect not the gift that is in thee, which was given thee by prophecy, with the laying on of the hands of the presbytery. (15) Meditate upon these things; give thyself wholly to them; that thy profiting may appear to all.

2 Timothy 1:6 – Wherefore I put thee in remembrance that thou stir up the gift of God, which is in thee by the putting on of my hands.

Hebrews 6:1-2 – (1) Therefore leaving the principles of the doctrine of Christ, let us go on unto perfection, not laying again the foundation of ... (2) laying on of hands.

* * * *

Note: In the Qur'an there is no mention of the laying on of hands for the impartation of spiritual gifts. cf. Rom. 1:11; 1 Tim. 4:14-16.

58

Does God give the followers of Jesus the ability to do the same kind of miracles that Jesus did through the power of the Holy Spirit dwelling within them?

^{Bible} **Yes** / **No** ^{Qur'an}

Luke 10:17 – And the seventy returned again with joy, saying, Lord, even the devils are subject unto us through thy name.

John 14:12 – Verily, verily, I say unto you, He that believeth on me, the works that I do shall he do also; and greater works than these shall he do, because I go unto my Father.

Acts 6:8 – And Stephen, full of faith and power, did great wonders and miracles among the people.

Acts 8:6 – The people with one accord gave heed unto those things which Philip spake, hearing and seeing the miracles which he did.

Acts 9:36-41 – (36) Tabitha... (37) was sick and died... (40) Peter put them all forth, and kneeled down, and prayed; and turning to the body said, Tabitha arise. And she opened her eyes.

Acts 28:8 – the father of Publius lay sick of a fever... Paul entered in, and prayed, and laid hands on him, and healed him.

* * * *

Note: There are no records found in the Qur'an of anyone doing any obvious miracles after Jesus.

59

Does God give some believers the gift of speaking in an unknown tongue or language through the power of the Holy Spirit?

Bible **Yes** / **No** Qur'an

Jude 1:20-21 – (20) But ye, beloved, building up yourselves on your most holy faith, praying in the Holy Spirit, (21) keep yourselves in the love of God looking for the mercy of our Lord Jesus Christ unto eternal life.

Romans 8:26 – (26) Likewise the Spirit also helpeth our infirmities: for we know not what we should pray for as we ought: but the Spirit itself maketh intercession for us with groanings which cannot be uttered.

1 Corinthians 14:2, 5, 11-12, 26-27 – (2) For he that speaketh in an unknown tongue speaketh not unto men, but unto God: for no man understandeth him; howbeit in the spirit he speaketh mysteries ... (26-27) How is it then, brethren? when ye come together, every one of you hath a psalm, hath a doctrine, hath a tongue, hath a revelation, hath an interpretation. Let all things be done unto edifying. If any man speak in an unknown tongue, let it be by two, or at the most by three, and that by course; and let one interpret.

* * * *

Note: In the Qur'an there are no verses about speaking in tongues.

60

Is there a clear-cut distinction between angels (Melek) being the servants of God and Demons (Jinn) being the servants of Satan?

^{Bible} **Yes** / **No** ^{Qur'an}

Matthew 25:41 – Then he shall say also unto them on the left hand, Depart from me, ye cursed, into everlasting fire, prepared for the devil and his angels.

2 Peter 2:4 – For if God spared not the angels that sinned, but cast them down to hell...

Revelation 12:9 – And the great dragon was cast out, that old serpent, called the Devil, and Satan, which deceiveth the whole world; he was cast out into the earth, and his angels were cast out with him.

Jinn 72:1-16 – (1) Say (O Muhammad): "It has been revealed to me that a company of the jinn gave ear, and said: 'We have heard a wonderful Qur'an, (2) Which guides to righteousness, so we believe in it and we shall not join (in worship) any (gods) with our Lord ... (11) And among us are righteous folk and among us there are far from that. We are sects having different rules. (13) And when we heard the guidance, we believed in it: he that believes in his Lord shall fear neither wrong nor harm. (14) Among us there are some who have surrendered (to Allah) and there are some who are unjust.' Now those who surrendered to Allah, such have taken the right path." ...

61

Would it be possible for Satan to repent and become good?

^{Bible} **No / No** ^{Qur'an}

Matthew 25:41 – Depart from me, ye cursed, into everlasting fire, prepared for the devil and his angels.

2 Peter 2:4 – For if God spared not the angels that sinned, but cast them down to hell, and delivered them into chains of darkness, to be reserved unto judgment.

Revelation 12:9 – And the great dragon was cast out, that old serpent, called the Devil, and Satan, who deceiveth the whole world; he was cast out into the earth, and his angels were cast out with him.

Revelation 20:10 – And the devil that deceived them was cast into the lake of fire and brimstone ... and shall be tormented day and night forever and ever.

Bakara 2:208 – Do not walk in Satan's footsteps; assuredly he is an open enemy to you.

Yusuf 12:5 – Satan is an open enemy to man.

Zukhruf 43:36-39 – (36) We set a devil upon him, who becomes his comrade. (39) (Then it will be said to them): "Now you have done wrong, it avails you nothing today that (you and your satans) are partners in the torment."

62

Would it be possible for some Demons to repent and become good? (Jinn)

^{Bible} **No** / **Yes** ^{Qur'an}

Matthew 25:41 – Then shall he say... Depart from me, ye cursed, into everlasting fire, prepared for the devil and his angels.

Jude 6-7 – (6) And the angels which kept not their first estate, but left their own habitation, he hath reserved in everlasting chains under darkness unto the judgment of the great day. (7) Are set forth for an example, suffering the vengeance of eternal fire.

Ahkaf 46:29-31 – (29) We brought to you a group of jinn so that they might listen to the Qur'an. (30) It confirms what came before it, and it guides to the Truth and to a Straight Road.

Jinn 72:1, 11, 13, 14 – (1) Say O Muhammad: 'It has been revealed to me that a company of the jinn gave ear,' and they said: We have heard a wonderful Qur'an. (11) And among us there are righteous folk and among us there are far from that. We are sects having different rules. (13) And when we heard the guidance, we believed in it: he that believes in his Lord shall fear neither wrong nor harm. (14) Among us there are some who have surrendered to Allah and there are among us some who are unjust.

63

Are there verses in the Holy Books about casting demons out of people?

^{Bible} **Yes** / **No** ^{Qur'an}

Matthew 9:33 – And when the devil was cast out, the dumb spake; and the multitudes marvelled, saying, It was never so seen in Israel.

Matthew 17:18 – Jesus rebuked the devil, and he departed out of him; and the child was cured.

Mark 1:25-26 – (25) And Jesus rebuked him, saying, Hold thy peace, and come out of him. (26) And when the unclean spirit had torn him, and cried with a loud voice, he came out of him.

Mark 5:1-13 – (6) Jesus… (8) Come out of the man, thou unclean spirit… (13) And the unclean spirits went out, and entered into the swine.

Luke 4:35 – (35) And Jesus rebuked him, saying, Hold thy peace, and come out of him. And when the devil had thrown him in the midst, he came out of him, and hurt him not. cf. Luke 8:33; 9:42.

* * * *

Note: There are no verses in the Qur'an about casting demons out of people; but there are 89 verses in the Bible about the casting out of demons.

64

Is Satan's power of deception depicted as being weak or ineffective?

^{Bible} **No / Yes** ^{Qur'an}

Luke 4:6 – And the devil said unto him, All this power will I give thee, and the glory of them; for that is delivered unto me, and to whomsoever I will I give it.

2 Corinthians 4:3-4 – (3) If our gospel be hid ... (4) the god of this world hath blinded the minds of them which believe not.

Revelation 12:9 – And the great dragon was cast out, that old serpent, called the Devil and Satan, which deceiveth the whole world; he was cast out into the earth, and his angels were cast out with him.

Nisâ 4:76 – Assuredly, the devil's strategy is ever weak.

İbrahim 14:22 – Satan will say ... I had no power over you except to call you.

Nahl 16:98-99 – (98) When you recite the Qur'an seek refuge in Allah from Satan the accursed. (99) He has no power over those who believe and put their trust in their Lord.

Isra 17:62-65 – (62) İblis... (65) over my (true) servants you shall have no power.

Shu'arâ 26:210-211 – (210) The devils did not bring it down. (211) It is not meet for them, nor is it in their power.

65

Is Satan considered to be the prince or ruler of this world?

^{Bible} **Yes** / **No** ^{Qur'an}

Luke 4:6 – And the devil said unto him, All this power will I give thee ... for that is delivered unto me, and to whomsoever I will I give it.

John 12:31 – Now is the judgment of this world; now shall the prince of this world be cast out.

John 14:30 – Hereafter ... the prince of this world cometh, and hath nothing in me.

John 16:11 – The prince of this world is judged.

2 Corinthians 4:3-4 – (3) But if our gospel be hid, it is hid to them that are lost: (4) In whom the god of this world hath blinded the minds of them which believe not.

2 Corinthians 11:14 – And no marvel; for Satan himself is transformed into an angel of light.

Nisa 4:76 – The devil's strategy is ever weak.

İbrahim 14:22 – Satan will say: "I too promised, but failed in my promise to you. I had no power over you except to call you, but you listened to me..."

Shuara 26:210-211 – (210) The devils did not bring it down, (211) nor is it in their power.

Christ and Muhammad

66

Is it accepted that Christ was born of a virgin?

^{Bible} **Yes** / **Yes** ^{Qur'an}

Isaiah 7:14 – Therefore the Lord himself shall give you a sign; Behold, the virgin shall conceive, and bear a son, and shall call his name Immanuel.

Matthew 1:18-21 – (18) Now the birth of Jesus Christ was on this wise: When, as his mother, Mary, was espoused to Joseph, before they came together, she was found with child of the Holy Ghost... (20) an angel of the Lord appeared unto him in a dream, saying, Joseph... that which is conceived in her is of the Holy Ghost. (21) And she shall bring forth a son, and thou shalt call his name JESUS; for he shall save his people from their sins. (22) Now all this was done, that it might be fulfilled which was spoken of the Lord by the prophet, saying, Behold the virgin shall be with child, and shall bring forth a son, and they shall call his name Emmanuel, which being interpreted is, God with us.

Meryem 19:16-22 – (16) Mary ... (20) said: "How can I have a son when no man has touched me; neither have I been unchaste?" (21) (The angel) replied, "So shall it be; your Lord says: 'This is an easy thing for Me ... (22) And We shall make him a sign for mankind and a blessing from Us.' It is a matter decreed.

Enbiya 21:91 – We breathed into her of Our spirit, and We made her and her son a sign for all peoples.

67

Is it accepted that Christ was sinless?

^{Bible} **Yes** / **Yes** ^{Qur'an}

Mark 1:24 – Jesus ... the Holy One of God.

John 7:18 – He that seeketh his glory that sent him, the same is true, and no unrighteousness is in him.

John 8:46 – Which of you convinceth me of sin? And if I say the truth, why do ye not believe me?

2 Corinthians 5:21 – For he hath made him to be sin for us, who knew no sin.

1 Peter 1:18-19 – (18) Forasmuch as ye know that ye were not redeemed with corruptible things, as silver and gold, from your vain conversation received by tradition from your fathers; (19) But with the precious blood of Christ, as of a lamb without blemish and without spot:

1 Peter 2:21-22 – (21) Christ ... (22) who did no sin, neither was guile found in his mouth.

1 John 3:5 – And ye know that he was manifested to take away our sins, and in him is no sin.

Bakara 2:253 – We gave Jesus Son of Mary clear signs and strengthened him with the Holy Spirit.

Meryem 19:19 – He said; "I am only a messenger of your Lord to announce to you the gift of a pure son."

68

Is it accepted that Christ possessed supernatural wisdom and knowledge?

^{Bible} **Yes / Yes** ^{Qur'an}

Matthew 9:4 – Jesus, knowing their thoughts, said, Wherefore think ye evil in your hearts?

Matthew 24:3, 25 – (3) Tell us, when shall these things be? And what shall be the sign of thy coming, and of the end of the world?... (25) Behold I have told you before.

John 2:24-25 – (24) But Jesus did not commit himself unto them, because he knew all men... (25) for he knew what was in man...

John 7:45-46 – (45) Why have ye not brought him? (46) The officers answered, Never man spake like this man.

John 16:30 – Now are we sure that thou knowest all things ... by this we believe that thou camest forth from God.

Al-i İmran 3:45-48 – (45) The Messiah, Jesus ... one of those who shall be brought near to God, (48) And he will teach him the Scripture and wisdom, and the Torah and the Gospel.

Zukhruf 43:63 – And when Jesus came with clear proofs of Allah's sovereignty, he said: "I have brought wisdom to you, and have come to make plain to you the reality of those things in which you differ: so fear Allah and obey me."

69

Is it accepted that Christ possessed supernatural power to do miracles and give life to the dead?

^{Bible} **Yes** / **Yes** ^{Qur'an}

Mark 1:40-45 – (40) And there came a leper ... If thou wilt, thou canst make me clean. (41) Jesus ... saith unto him, I will; be thou clean.

Mark 6:48 – He cometh unto them, walking upon the sea.

John 11:14-44 – (14) Then said Jesus unto them plainly, Lazarus is dead. (25) Jesus said unto her, I am the resurrection and the life. (43) He cried with a loud voice, Lazarus come forth. (44) And he that was dead came forth.

Al-i İmran 3:45-50 – (45) The Messiah, Jesus ... (49) By Allah's leave I shall give sight to the blind, heal the leper, and raise the dead to life.

Maide 5:110 – You did heal him who was born blind and the leper by My permission; and how you did raise the dead, by My permission.

* * * *

Note: There are 37 miracles of Jesus in the Injil.

70

Is it accepted that Christ is entitled to command faith and obedience from all men?

^{Bible} **Yes** / **Yes** ^{Qur'an}

Matthew 23:10 – For one is your Master, even Christ.

Luke 8:25 – What manner of man is this! For he commandeth even the winds and water, and they obey him.

John 8:51 – If a man keep my saying, he shall never see death...

John 12:48 – He that rejecteth me, and receiveth not my words, hath one that judgeth him: the word that I have spoken, the same shall judge him in the last day.

John 14:15, 21-24 – (15) If ye love me, keep my commandments. (21) He that hath my commandments, and keepeth them, he it is that loveth me ... (23) If a man love me, he will keep my words ... (24) He that loveth me not keepeth not my sayings.

Al-i İmran 3:50, 55 – (50) I bring a sign to you from your Lord. So fear Him, and obey me. (55) I am gathering you and causing you to ascend to me ... and am setting those who follow you above those who disbelieve until the Day of resurrection.

Zukhruf 43:61, 63 – (61) And the second coming of Jesus shall be a sign of the Hour: therefore, do not have any doubt about it, and follow Me. This is the Straight Way. (63) I have brought wisdom to you ... so fear Allah and obey me.

71

Is it accepted that Jesus Christ is identified as being the Messiah? (the Anointed One)

Bible **Yes** / **Yes** Qur'an

Matthew 26:63-64 – (63) Tell us whether thou be the Christ, the Son of God. (64) Jesus saith unto him, Thou hast said.

John 1:41 – We have found the Messias, which is being interpreted, the Christ.

John 4:25-26 – (25) The woman saith unto him, I know that Messias cometh, which is called Christ; when he is come, he will tell us all things. (26) Jesus saith unto her, I that speak unto thee am he.

Al-i İmran 3:45 – Allah gives glad tidings of a word from Him, whose name is the Messiah, Jesus.

Nisa 4:171-172 – (171) The Messiah, Jesus son of Mary, was only a messenger of Allah ... (172) The Messiah will never disdain to be a slave of Allah.

* * * *

Note: The words *Messiah* or *Christ* are used 558 times in the New Testament and the word *Messiah* is used 11 times in the Qur'an to refer to Christ.

72

Is it accepted that Christ is referred to as the Word of God? (Logos / Kalimullâh)

^{Bible} **Yes** / **Yes** ^{Qur'an}

Micah 5:2 – But thou, Bethlehem... out of thee shall he come forth unto me that is to be ruler in Israel, whose goings forth have been from of old, from everlasting.

John 1:1-3, 14 – (1) In the beginning was the Word, and Word was with God, and the Word was God. (2) The same was in the beginning with God. (3) All things were made by him; and without him was not anything made that was made. (14) And the Word was made flesh, and dwelt among us.

John 6:51, 62 – (51) I am the living bread which came down from heaven... (62) What if ye shall see the Son of man ascend up where he was before?

Revelation 19:13-16 – (13) His name is called The Word of God. (16) KING OF KINGS, AND LORD OF LORDS.

Al-i İmran 3:39 – Allah gives you the glad tidings of a son whose name is John, who comes to confirm a word from Allah, princely and chaste, a Prophet of the righteous.

Al-i İmran 3:45 – Allah gives glad tidings of a word from Him, whose name is the Messiah, Jesus ... one of those who shall be brought near to God.

73

Is it accepted that Christ pre-existed as the Word of God before he was born?

^{Bible} **Yes / No** ^{Qur'an}

Isaiah 9:6 – For unto us a child is born ... and his name shall be called ... The mighty God, The everlasting Father.

Micah 5:2 – But thou, Bethlehem ... out of thee shall he come forth ... whose goings forth have been from of old, from everlasting.

John 8:58 – Jesus said unto them, Verily, verily, I say unto you, Before Abraham was, I am.

John 17:5, 16 – (5) And now, O Father, glorify thou me with thine own self with the glory which I had with thee before the world was… (16) I am not of the world.

Hebrews 13:8 – Jesus Christ, the same yesterday, and today, and forever.

Revelation 1:1, 8, 17 – (1) The Revelation of Jesus Christ… (8) I am the Alpha and Omega, the beginning and the ending, saith the Lord, which is, and which was, and which is to come… (17) I am the first and the last…

Al-i İmran 3:59 – The likeness of Jesus with Allah is as the likeness of Adam. He created him of dust, then He said to him: Be! And he was.

74

Is it accepted that God's eternal Word took on a human body in the incarnation of Jesus Christ? (Kenosis or Hûlul)

Bible **Yes** / **No** Qur'an

Matthew 1:18-24 – (23) Behold, a virgin shall be with child, and shall bring forth a son, and they shall call his name Emmanuel, which ... is God with us.

John 1:1, 14 – (1) In the beginning was the Word. (14) And the Word was made flesh, and dwelt among us.

Philippians 2:5-8 – (5) Christ Jesus, (6) Who, being in the form of God ... (7) was made in the likeness of men: (8) as a man, he humbled himself.

Colossians 1:3, 15 – (3) Our Lord Jesus Christ, (15) Who is the image of the invisible God.

1 Timothy 3:16 – God was manifest in the flesh.

Hebrews 2:14 – Forasmuch, then, as the children are partakers of flesh and blood, he also himself likewise took part of the same, that through death he might destroy him that had the power of death, that is the devil.

Maide 5:17 – They indeed have disbelieved who say: "Allah is the Messiah, son of Mary" ... Allah creates what He will.

75

Is it accepted that Christ is Divine or God in the flesh?

^{Bible} **Yes** / **No** ^{Qur'an}

John 1:1, 14 – (1) In the beginning was the Word, and the Word was with God, and the Word was God. (14) And the Word was made flesh, and dwelt among us.

John 5:17-18 – (17) Jesus answered them, My Father worketh hitherto, and I work. (18) He ... said ... God was his Father, making himself equal with God.

John 10:25-33 – (25) Jesus answered them ... the works that I do in my Father's name, they bear witness of me. (30) I and my Father are one.

John 20:28-29 – (28) Thomas answered, ... My Lord and my God. (29) Jesus saith unto him ... blessed are they that have not seen, and yet have believed.

Colossians 2:8-9 – (8) Christ: (9) For in him dwelleth all the fullness of the Godhead bodily.

Maide 5:17, 72, 75, 116 – (17) They indeed have disbelieved who say: "Allah is the Messiah."

Zukhruf 43:57-59 – (57) The son of Mary ... (59) He is nothing but a slave whom We rendered an example.

* * * *

Note: The Bible depicts Jesus as God 367 times.

76

Is it accepted that Christ created the world?

Bible **Yes** / **No** Qur'an

John 1:1-4, 10, 14 – (1) In the beginning was the Word, and Word was with God, and the Word was God. (2) The same was in the beginning with God. (3) All things were made by him; and without him was not anything made that was made... (10) He was in the world and the world was made by him, and the world knew him not... (14) And the Word was made flesh, and dwelt among us and we beheld his glory, the glory as of the only begotten of the Father, full of grace and truth.

Ephesians 3:9 – God, who created all things by Jesus Christ.

Colossians 1:13-20 – (13) The kingdom of his dear Son: (15) Who is the image of the invisible God, (16) For by him were all things created, that are in heaven, and that are in earth.

Hebrews 1:1-2, 10-12 – (1) God ... (2) Hath in these last days spoken unto us by his Son ... by whom also he made the worlds; (10) Thou ... hast laid the foundation of the earth.

Maide 5:75 – (75) The messiah, son of Mary, was no other than a messenger.

Zukhruf 43:59 – Jesus is nothing but a slave whom We rendered an example for the Children of Israel.

77

Is it accepted that Christ is the one and only mediator between God and man?

^{Bible} **Yes** / **No** ^{Qur'an}

John 14:6 – Jesus saith ... I am the way, the truth, and the life; no man cometh unto the Father, but by me.

Acts 4:12 – Neither is there salvation in any other; for there is no other name under heaven given among men, whereby we must be saved.

Romans 8:34 – Christ... who is even at the right hand of God, who also maketh intercession for us.

1 Timothy 2:5-6 – (5) For there is one God, and one mediator between God and men, the man Christ Jesus; (6) Who gave himself a ransom for all.

Hebrews 9:15 – for this cause he is the mediator...

Hebrews 12:24 – Jesus, the mediator of the new covenant.

Bakara 2:48 – And guard yourselves against a day when no soul shall aid another, and no intercession or ransom, or any compensation shall be accepted from it.

Yunus 10:3 – Allah ... there is no intercessor (with Him)

Zümer 39:44 – Intercession is wholly in the power of Allah.

78

Is it accepted that Christ is the Son of God?

^{Bible} **Yes** / **No** ^{Qur'an}

Matthew 16:16-17 – Simon Peter answered and said, Thou art the Christ, the Son of the living God. (17) Jesus answered and said unto him, Blessed art thou, Simon.

Mark 14:61-62 – (61) Art thou the Christ, the Son of the Blessed? (62) And Jesus said, I am.

Luke 1:32, 35 – (32) He shall be great, and shall be called the Son of the Highest. (35) Therefore also that holy thing which shall be born of thee shall be called the Son of God.

John 1:29-34 – (29) John seeth Jesus ... (34) I saw, and bare record that this is the Son of God.

Tevbe 9:30-31 – (30) The Christians say the Messiah is the son of Allah. (31) May God assail them. How perverse they are! Transcendent is He above what they associate with Him.

Furkan 25:2 – No son has He begotten... No partner has He in His sovereignty!

* * * *

Note: There are 92 verses in the Bible which depict Jesus as "The Son of God"; but cf. En'am 6:101; Jinn 72:3.

79

In the Holy Books when the term "Son of God" is used, is it used in the sense of a physical son being born from out of a sexual union?

^{Bible} **No / Yes** ^{Qur'an}

Isaiah 7:14 – Therefore the LORD himself shall give you a sign; Behold, the virgin shall conceive, and bear a son, and shall call his name Immanuel.

Isaiah 9:6 – unto us a son is given, and... his name shall be called... The Mighty God, The Everlasting Father, The Prince of Peace.

Luke 1:26-35 – (27) The virgin's name was Mary. (35) The Holy Ghost shall come upon thee, and the power of the Highest shall overshadow thee; therefore also that holy thing which shall be born of thee shall be called the Son of God.

1 John 5:20 – And we know that the Son of God is come, and hath given us an understanding, that we may know him that is true ... This is the true God, and eternal life.

En'am 6:101 – The Originator of the heavens and the earth! How can He have a child, when there is for Him no consort, when He created all things and is Aware of all things?

Jinn 72:3 – And we believe that He ... has taken neither wife nor son.

80

Was Christ actually worshipped by people and did He accept their worship as being valid?

^{Bible} **Yes / No** ^{Qur'an}

Matthew 28:9-10 – (9) Jesus met them… and they came and held him by the feet and they and worshipped him… (10) Then said Jesus unto them, Be not afraid; go tell my brethren…

John 9:35-38 – (35) Dost thou believe on the Son of God? (38) Lord I believe. And he worshipped him.

John 20:28-29 – (28) Thomas answered … My Lord and my God. (29) Jesus saith … blessed are they that have not seen, and yet have believed.

Philippians 2:10-11 – (10) At the name of Jesus every knee should bow … (11) and that every tongue confess that Jesus Christ is Lord.

Hebrews 1:6 – And again when he bringeth in the first-begotten into the world, he saith, let all of the angels of God worship him.

Maide 5:116, 118 – (116) And when Allah said: "O Jesus, son of Mary!" Did you say to mankind: "Take me and my mother for two gods beside Allah?" he said: "Be glorified! It was not mine to say that to which I had no right." (118) You, only You, are the Mighty, the Wise.

81

Is it accepted that Christ can forgive people's sins?

^{Bible} **Yes** / **No** ^{Qur'an}

Mark 2:5-7, 10-11 – (5) When Jesus saw their faith, he said unto the sick of the palsy, Son, thy sins are forgiven thee ... (7) Why doth this man thus speak blasphemies? Who can forgive sins but God only? (10) But that ye may know that the Son of man hath power on earth to forgive sins ... (11) I say unto thee, Arise, and take up thy bed, and go thy way.

Luke 5:20 – And when he saw their faith, he said unto him, Man, thy sins are forgiven thee.

Luke 7:48 – He said ... Thy sins are forgiven.

Acts 10:43 – To him give all the prophets witness, that through his name whosoever believeth in him shall receive remission of sins.

Acts 13:38 – Through this man is preached unto you the forgiveness of sins.

1 John 2:12 – I write unto you ... because your sins are forgiven you for his name's sake.

Al-i İmran 3:135 – Who can forgive sins except Allah only?

Maide 5:75 – The messiah, son of Mary, was no other than a messenger.

82

Is it accepted that Christ has the keys to death and hell?

^{Bible} **Yes** / **No** ^{Qur'an}

Luke 12:5 – But I will forewarn you whom ye shall fear; Fear him which, after he hath killed, hath power to cast into hell; yea... Fear him.

Revelation 1:1-18 – (1) The Revelation of Jesus Christ ... (5) And from Jesus Christ, who is the faithful witness, and the first begotten of the dead, and the prince of the kings of the earth. Unto him that loved us, and washed us from our sins in his own blood ... (8) I am Alpha and Omega, the beginning and the ending, saith the Lord, which is, and which was, and which is to come, the Almighty ... (14) His eyes were as a flame of fire; (17) I am the first and the last; (18) I am he that liveth, and was dead; and behold, I am alive for evermore, Amen, and have the keys of hell and of death.

Maide 5:75 – The messiah, son of Mary, was no other than a messenger...

Zukhruf 43:57, 59 – (57) The son of Mary ... (59) He is nothing but a slave whom We rendered an example for the Children of Israel.

83

Is it accepted that Christ is the Saviour of the world?

^{Bible} **Yes** / **No** ^{Qur'an}

Isaiah 43:11-13 – (11) I, even I, am the LORD, and beside me there is no saviour ... (13) Yea ... I am he.

Luke 2:11 – For unto you is born this day in the city of David a Saviour, which is Christ the Lord.

John 4:42 – Know that this is indeed the Christ, the Saviour of the world.

Acts 13:23 – Of this man's seed hath God, according to his promise, raised unto Israel a Saviour Jesus.

Titus 1:3-4 – (3) God our Saviour... (4) Grace, mercy, and peace, from God, the Father, and the Lord Jesus Christ, our Saviour...

Titus 3:4-6 – (4) But after the kindness and love of God our Saviour ... (6) which he shed on us abundantly through Jesus Christ, our Saviour.

1 John 4:14 – We have seen and do testify that the Father sent the Son to be the Saviour of the world.

Nisa 4:171 – The Messiah, Jesus son of Mary, was only a messenger of Allah.

Maide 5:75 – The messiah, son of Mary, was no other than a messenger, messengers the like of whom had passed away before him.

84

Is it accepted that believing in Christ as Saviour and Lord is the only means of obtaining eternal life?

^{Bible} **<u>Yes</u> / <u>No</u>** ^{Qur'an}

John 3:16, 36 – (16) For God so loved the world, that he gave his only begotten Son, that whosoever believeth in him should not perish, but have everlasting life. (36) He that believeth on the Son hath everlasting life … He that believeth not the Son shall not see life, but the wrath of God abideth on him.

John 11:25-26 – (25) Jesus… I am the resurrection, and the life; he that believeth in me, though he were dead, yet shall he live. (26) And whosoever liveth and believeth in me shall never die…

John 14:6 – Jesus saith unto him, I am the way, the truth, and the life; no man cometh unto the Father, but by me.

Acts 4:10-12 – (10) By the name of Jesus Christ … (12) Neither is there salvation in any other; for there is no other name under heaven given among men, whereby we must be saved.

Al-i İmran 3:19, 85 – (19) The true religion in the sight of Allah is Islam. (85) He who seeks a religion other than Islam, it will not be accepted from him, and he will be a loser in the Hereafter.

* * * *

Note: There are over 200 verses in the Bible which depict Jesus as being the Saviour of the world.

85

Is it accepted that Christ's blood was shed as a sacrificial atonement for the sins of the world?

^{Bible} **Yes / No** ^{Qur'an}

Isaiah 53:5-12 – (5) But he was wounded for our transgressions, he was bruised for our iniquities ... and with his stripes we are healed. (6) ... and the Lord hath laid on him the iniquity of us all.

John 1:29 – John ... saith, Behold the Lamb of God, which taketh away the sin of the world.

1 Corinthians 5:7 – For even Christ, our Passover, is sacrificed for us...

1 Corinthians 15:3-4 – (3) Christ died for our sins according the scriptures; (4) And that he was buried, and that he rose again the third day according to the scriptures.

Hebrews 9:11-12, 22 – (11) Christ... (12) by his own blood he entered in once into the holy place, having obtained eternal redemption for us... (22) And almost all things are by the law purged with blood, and without shedding of blood is no remission.

En'am 6:164 – Each soul earns only on its own account, nor do any laden bear another's load.

İsra 17:15 – No soul can bear another's burden.

Nejm 53:38 – No soul shall bear another's burden.

86

In the Holy Books is it stated by the prophets that the Messiah (Jesus) would die?

^{Bible} **Yes / Yes** ^{Qur'an}

Psalms 16:10 – Thou wilt not leave my soul in hell; neither wilt thou suffer thine Holy One to see corruption.

Isaiah 53:1-12 – (8) For he was cut off out of the land of the living; for the transgression of my people he was stricken. (9) And he made his grave with the wicked, and with the rich in his death... (10) When thou shalt make his soul an offering for sin... (11) for he shall bear their iniquities... (12) he hath poured out his soul unto death; and he was numbered with the transgressors; and he bore the sin of many, and made intercession for the transgressors.

Daniel 9:26 – After threescore and two weeks shall Messiah be cut off, but not for himself.

Al-i İmran 3:55 – God said: "O Jesus! Verily I shall cause thee to die, and shalt exalt thee unto Me, and cleanse thee of (the presence of) those who are bent on denying the truth. (Muhammad Asad)

Meryem 19:30, 33 – (30) He has given me the Scripture and has appointed me a prophet. (33) So peace be upon me the day that I was born and the day that I die and the day that I shall be raised up to life (again).

87

Did Jesus himself foretell that he would be killed by the Jews?

^{Bible} **Yes** / **No** ^{Qur'an}

Matthew 16:21 – From that time forth began Jesus to shew unto his disciples, how that he must go unto Jerusalem, and suffer many things of the elders and chief priests and scribes, and be killed, and be raised again the third day.

John 2:18-21 – Destroy this temple, and in three days I will raise it up... But he spake of the temple of his body.

John 10:11, 15, 17, 18 – (11) I am the good shepherd; the good shepherd giveth his life for the sheep... (15) I lay down my life for the sheep... (17) I lay down my life, that I might take it again. (18) No man taketh it from me, but I lay it down of myself. I have power to lay it down, and I have power to take it again.

John 12:32-33 – (32) And I, if I be lifted up from the earth, will draw all men unto me ... (33) This he said, signifying what death he should die.

* * * *

Note: In the Qur'an there are no verses where Jesus said that he would be killed by the Jews.

88

Is it accepted that Christ physically died on the cross and that he arose from the dead?

^{Bible} **Yes** / **No** ^{Qur'an}

Matthew 27:50 – Jesus, when he had cried again with a loud voice, yielded up the ghost.

Mark 15:37 – And Jesus cried with a loud voice, and gave up the ghost.

Luke 24:44, 46 – (44) All things must be fulfilled which were written in the law of Moses, and in the prophets, and in the psalms concerning me. (46) Thus it is written, and thus it behooved Christ to suffer, and to rise from the dead.

John 19:30 – Jesus ... said, It is finished; and he bowed his head, and gave up the spirit.

Acts 3:14-15 – (14) ye denied the Holy One and the Just, and desired a murderer... (15) and killed the Prince of life, whom God hath raised from the dead, whereof we are witnesses.

1 Corinthians 15:3-4 – (3) Christ died for our sins according to the scriptures; (4) and that he was buried, and that he rose again.

Nisa 4:157 – They slew him not, nor crucified him, but it appeared so to them; and those who disagree concerning it are in doubt thereof; they have no knowledge thereof except pursuit of a conjecture; they slew him not for certain.

89

Is it accepted that Christ is alive today and that he will come again?

^{Bible} **Yes / Yes** ^{Qur'an}

John 14:2-3 – (2) In my Father's house are many mansions ... I go to prepare a place for you. (3) And if I go and prepare a place for you, I will come again, and receive you unto myself.

Titus 2:13 – Looking for that blessed hope, and the glorious appearing of the great God and our Savior, Jesus Christ.

Revelation 2:25 – But that which ye have already hold fast till I come.

Revelation 22:12, 20 – (12) And behold, I come quickly, and my reward is with me, to give every man according as his work shall be. (20) Surely, I come quickly. Amen. Even so, come, Lord Jesus.

Nisa 4:158 – Allah raised him up to Himself.

Zukhruf 43:61 – And (the second coming of Jesus shall be) a sign of the Hour: therefore, do not have any doubt about it.

* * * *

Note: There are 73 verses in the Bible about the second coming of Christ. cf. Bukhari Vol. 4, no. 657.

90

Are there any verses in the Bible which predict or foretell the coming of Muhammad?

^{Bible} **No / Yes** ^{Qur'an}

Matthew 7:15-20 – (15) Beware of false prophets… (20) Wherefore, by their fruits ye shall know them.

Matthew 24:11, 24-26 – (11) many false prophets shall rise, and shall deceive many… (24) for there shall arise false Christs, and false prophets… (25) behold I have told you before… (26) Wherefore if they shall say unto you, Behold, he is in the desert… believe it not.

Luke 24:27 – And beginning at Moses and all the prophets, he expounded unto them, in all the scriptures, the things concerning himself.

John 5:31 – If I bear witness of myself, my witness is not true.

2 Corinthians 13:1 – In the mouth of two or three witnesses shall every word be established.

A'raf 7:157 – Those who follow the messenger, the prophet who can neither read nor write, whom they find described in the Torah and Gospel.

Saf 61:6 – Jesus … said … I am the messenger of Allah to you, confirming that which was revealed before me in the Torah (Books of Moses) and bringing good tidings of a messenger who will come after me, whose name is Ahmed.

91

In order for Muhammad to be qualified as a prophet to communicate the written oracles of God, would he have needed to be a Jew who was literate?

Bible **Yes** / **No** Qur'an

Genesis 12:1-3 – (1) The LORD said unto Abram... (2) I will make of thee a great nation, and I will bless thee, and make thy name great, and thou shalt be a blessing... (3) in thee shall all families of the earth be blessed.

John 4:22 – Salvation is of the Jews.

Romans 3:1-2 – (1) What advantage, then, hath the Jew? Or what profit is there of circumcision? (2) Much every way, chiefly because unto them were committed the oracles of God.

Romans 9:3-4 – (3) For I wish that I myself were accursed from Christ for my brethren, my kinsmen according to the flesh... (4) who are the Israelites to whom pertaineth: adoption, glory, covenants, giving of the law, service of God, and the promises..

A'raf 7:157-158 – (157) Those who follow the messenger, the prophet who can neither read nor write ... (158) So believe in Allah and His messenger the prophet who can neither read nor write.

Shura 42:52 – And thus We have (O Muhammad) revealed a Spirit to you by Our Command. You did not know what was the Scripture.

92

Is Muhammad's self-proclamation of being a prophet a valid test or proof of prophethood?

_{Bible} **No / Yes** _{Qur'an}

Deuteronomy 19:15 – One witness shall not rise up… at the mouth of two witnesses, or at the mouth of three witnesses, shall the matter be established.

John 5:31, 36 – (31) If I bear witness of myself, my witness is not true. (36) The same works that I do, bear witness of me that the Father hath sent me.

1 Corinthians 14:32-33 – (32) And the spirits of the prophets are subject to the prophets. (33) For God is not the author of confusion but of peace.

2 Corinthians 13:1 – In the mouth of two or three witnesses shall every word be established.

Nisa 4:79 – We have sent you (Muhammad) as a Messenger to mankind. And Allah is sufficient as witness.

Rad 13:43 – Disbelievers… "You are not a messenger of (Allah)." Say: "Allah, and those who have knowledge of the Book, are sufficient witness between me and you.

Fetih 48:28 – He it is Who has sent His Messenger with guidance and the religion of truth, that He may cause it to prevail over all religion. And Allah is enough for a witness.

93

Was the message of Muhammad in complete agreement with the message of Jesus and the other prophets?

^{Bible} **No / Yes** ^{Qur'an}

Isaiah 8:20 – If they speak not according to this word, it is because there is no light in them.

1 Corinthians 14:32-33 – (32) And the spirits of the prophets are subject to the prophets. (33) For God is not the author of confusion, but of peace.

2 Thessalonians 3:6, 14 – (6) withdraw yourselves from every brother that... walketh not after the tradition which he received from us... (14) if any man obey not our word by this epistle, note that man, and have no company with him.

1 John 5:20 – And we know that the Son of God is come ... Jesus Christ. This is the true God.

Shu'ara 26:192-197 – (192) And verily it is a revelation of the Lord of the Worlds ... (196) And it is in the Scriptures of the men of old. (197) Is it not a sign for them that the doctors of the Children of Israel know it?

Fussilet 41:43 – O Prophet, nothing is said to you that has not already been said to the Messengers before you.

Shura 42:15 – Say: "I believe in whatever Book Allah has sent down ... Let there be no argument between us.

94

Did God give Muhammad supernatural power to do obvious miracles like Jesus and the other prophets as a confirmation that he was sent by God?

^{Bible} **No / No** ^{Qur'an}

John 5:31, 36 – (31) If I bear witness of myself, my witness is not true… (36) the works that I do, bear witness of me that the Father hath sent me.

John 14:11 – Believe me that I am in the Father, and the Father in me; or else believe me for the very works' sake.

En'am 6:37-38 – (37) They say, "Why has no sign been sent down upon him from his Lord?" Say: "Allah is certainly able to send down a sign" … (38) We have neglected nothing in the Book.

Yunus 10:20 – They say, "Why has a sign not been sent down to him from his Lord?" The unseen belongs only to Allah. Then watch and wait; I too will wait with you.

Kamer 54:1-2 – (1) The hour (of judgment) is drawing near, and the moon is cleft in two. (2) Yet when they see a sign they turn away and say: "Prolonged magic."

* * * *

Note: There are 157 recorded miracles by Jesus and the other Prophets in the Bible but nothing similar to these in the Qur'an.

95

Did Muhammad have a prophetic gift to be able to predict or foretell the future like Jesus and the other prophets?

^{Bible} **No** / **No** ^{Qur'an}

Deuteronomy 18:22 – When a prophet speaketh in the name of the LORD, if the thing follow not, nor come to pass ... the prophet hath spoken it presumptuously; thou shalt not be afraid of him.

1 Samuel 9:9 – Beforetime in Israel, when a man went to enquire of God, thus he spake, Come, and let us go to the seer; for he that is now called a Prophet was beforetime called a Seer.

Isaiah 41:22 – Let them bring them forth, and shew us what shall happen ... or declare us things to come.

En'am 6:50 – Say O Muhammad, I say not to you that I possess the treasures of Allah, nor that I have knowledge of the Unseen.

A'raf 7:188 – Had I knowledge of the Unseen, I should have abundance of wealth, and adversity would not touch me. I am but a warner, and a bearer of glad tidings unto people who believe.

Ahkaf 46:9 – I do not know what shall befall you tomorrow or what shall befall me. I only follow that which is revealed to me.

Jinn 72:26-28 – (26) He alone knows the unseen, and does not reveal to anyone His secret. (27) Except to every messenger whom He has chosen, and then He sends down guardians who walk before him and behind him. (28) That he may know that they have indeed conveyed the message of their Lord.

96

Would the God of Abraham ever condone Muhammad's kissing the Black Stone at the Ka'ba or condone his honouring other Arab pagan deities?

Bible <u>**No**</u> / <u>**Yes**</u> Qur'an

Exodus 20:3-5 – (3) Thou shalt have no other gods before me … (5) Thou shalt not bow down thyself.

1 Kings 19:18 – Yet I have left me seven thousand in Israel, all the knees which have not bowed unto Baal, and every mouth which hath not kissed him.

2 Corinthians 6:14-17 – (14) Be ye not unequally yoked together with unbelievers… (15) what part hath he that believeth with an infidel? (16) And what agreement hath the temple of God with idols?… (17) Wherefore come out from among them, and be ye separate, saith the Lord, and touch not the unclean thing… saith the Lord Almighty.

Bakara 2:158 – Indeed, as-Safa and al-Marwah are among the symbols of Allah. So whoever makes Hajj to the House or performs 'umrah – there is no blame upon him for walking between them.

Nejm 53:18-20 – (19) Have you thought upon Al-Lat and al-Uzza. (20) And Manat, the third, the other?

* * * *

Note: cf. Hadith: Bukhari 2:667, 673-680; En'am 6:103-109.

97

Would Muhammad have been considered to be a normal human being who needed to repent and ask forgiveness for his sins?

^{Bible} **Yes** / **Yes** ^{Qur'an}

Proverbs 20:9 – Who can say, I have made my heart clean, I am pure from my sin?

Ecclesiastes 7:20 – For there is not a just man upon earth, that doeth good and sinneth not.

Matthew 3:2, 8 – (2) Repent ye: for the kingdom of heaven is at hand. (8) Bring forth therefore fruits meet for repentance.

Matthew 9:12-13 – (12) Jesus ... (13) I am not come to call the righteous, but sinners to repentance.

1 John 1:8 – If we say that we have no sin, we deceive ourselves, and the truth is not in us.

Nisa 4:106 – And seek forgiveness of Allah.

Yusuf 12:53 – I do not ever free my own self of blame, the human soul is certainly prone to evil.

Muhammad 47:19 – Ask forgiveness for your fault.

* * * *

Note: Muhammad was not certain of his own salvation: cf. Ahkaf 46:9; Hadith: Bukhari Vol. 5, no. 266, 234-236.

98

Would Muhammad be considered to be the last and the greatest of the prophets?

^{Bible} **No / Yes** ^{Qur'an}

Revelation 1:1, 5, 8 – (1) The Revelation of Jesus Christ... (5) From Jesus Christ, who is the faithful witness, and the first begotten of the dead, and the prince of the kings of the earth. Unto him that loveth us, and washed us from our sins in his own blood... (8) I am the Alpha and the Omega, the beginning and the ending, saith the Lord, who is, and who was, and who is to come, the Almighty...

Revelation 22:13, 16, 20 – (13) I am Alpha and Omega, the beginning and the end, the first and the last. (16) I am ... the bright and morning star. (20) Surely I come quickly. Amen. Even so, come, Lord Jesus.

Ahzab 33:40 – Muhammad is not the father of any man among you, but he is the messenger of Allah and the Seal of the Prophets; and Allah is Aware of all things.

Fatih 48:28 – He it is Who has sent His Messenger with guidance and the religion of truth, that He may cause it to prevail over all religion. And Allah is enough for a witness.

** * **

Note: Jesus is expected to return. Muhammad is not.

Man and Sin

99

When Adam and Eve sinned, did it cause a fundamental separation between God and man which resulted in a need for man to be saved from God's judgment against sin?

^{Bible} <u>Yes</u> / <u>No</u> ^{Qur'an}

Genesis 2:16-17 – (16) And the Lord God commanded the man, saying, Of every tree of the garden thou mayest freely eat; (17) But of the tree of the knowledge of good and evil, thou shalt not eat of it; for in the day that thou eatest thereof thou shalt surely die.

Genesis 3:17, 19 – Because thou has hearkened unto the voice of thy wife, and hast eaten of the tree, of which I commanded thee, saying, Thou shalt not eat of it: cursed is the ground for thy sake; in sorrow shalt thou eat of it all the days of thy life… for dust thou art, and unto dust shalt thou return.

Romans 5:12-19 – (12) Wherefore, as by one man sin entered into the world, and death by sin, and so death passed upon all men, for all have sinned. (19) For as by one man's disobedience many were made sinners, so by the obedience of one shall many be made righteous.

Bakara 2:35-38 – (35) We said: "O Adam! Dwell with your wife (Eve) in paradise, and eat of its fruits to your hearts' content, whenever you will, but never approach this tree, or you shall both become transgressors. (36) But Satan caused them to swerve from it (the Garden), and expelled them from their former state.

100

Are there verses about people being born with a sin nature? (Original Sin)

^{Bible} **Yes** / **No** ^{Qur'an}

Isaiah 64:6 – But we are all as an unclean thing, and all our righteousnesses are as filthy rags; and we all do fade as a leaf, and our iniquities, like the wind, have taken us away.

Jeremiah 10:23 – O LORD, I know that the way of man is not in himself; it is not in man that walketh to direct his steps.

Jeremiah 13:23 – Can the Ethiopian change his skin, or the leopard his spots? Then may ye also do good, that are accustomed to do evil.

Jeremiah 17:9 – The heart is deceitful above all things, and desperately wicked; who can know it?

Romans 3:23 – For all have sinned, and come short of the glory of God.

Taha 20:122 – Then his Lord chose him: He relented towards him, and rightly guided him.

Tin 95:4 – Surely We have created man in the most noble mould.

* * * *

Note: Islam denies the doctrine of "original sin."

101

Are all men including the prophets guilty of having committed sin? (Jesus excepted)

Bible **Yes** / **Yes** Qur'an

1 Kings 8:46 – If they sin against thee (for there is no man who sinneth not).

Psalm 130:3 – If thou, LORD, shouldest mark iniquities, O Lord, who shall stand?

Proverbs 20:9 – Who can say, I have made my heart clean, I am pure from my sin?

Ecclesiastes 7:20 – For there is not a just man upon earth, that doeth good, and sinneth not.

Romans 3:10 – There is none righteous, no, not one.

1 John 1:8 – If we say that we have no sin, we deceive ourselves, and the truth is not in us.

Yusuf 12:53 – I do not ever free my own self of blame, the human soul is certainly prone to evil.

İbrahim 14:34 – Surely man is a wrong-doer.

Nahl 16:61 – If Allah were to punish men for their wrongdoing, He would not leave on the earth a single living creature.

Shu'ara 26:82 – And who, I ardently hope, will forgive me my sin on the Day of Judgment.

Muhammad 47:19 – Ask forgiveness for your fault.

102

Was Mary, the mother of Jesus, considered to have any divine endowments and should she be venerated as the Mother of God?

^{Bible} **No / No** ^{Qur'an}

Exodus 34:14 – the LORD whose name is Jealous, is a jealous God.

Isaiah 42:8 – I am the LORD: that is my name; and my glory will I not give to another.

John 2:3-5 – (3) When they wanted wine, the mother of Jesus saith unto him, They have no wine. (4) Jesus saith unto her, Woman, what have I to do with thee? Mine hour is not yet come. (5) His mother saith ... Whatsoever he saith unto you, do it.

Revelation 22:8-9 – (8) I fell down to worship before the feet of the angel... (9) he saith unto me: "See thou do it not; for I am thy fellow servant, and of thy brethren, the prophets."

Al-i İmran 3:64 – Say: O people of the Scripture! Come to an agreement between us and you, that we shall worship none but Allah, that we assign no partner to Him, and that none of us shall take others for lords beside Allah.

İsra 17:23 – Your Lord has decreed that you worship none but Him.

Zariyat 51:56 – I created jinn and humankind only that they might worship me.

103

Does a man's sin separate him from a holy God, and as a natural consequence, is it understood that sinners are condemned to go to hell?

^{Bible} **Yes / Yes** ^{Qur'an}

Proverbs 9:17-18 – (17) Stolen waters are sweet, and bread eaten in secret is pleasant. (18) But he knoweth not that the dead are there, and that her guests are in the depths of hell.

Jeremiah 31:30 – every one shall die for his own iniquity.

Ezekiel 18:4, 20 – (4) The soul that sinneth, it shall die. (20) The soul that sinneth, it shall die.

Luke 12:5 – Fear him, which after he hath killed, hath power to cast into hell; yea ... Fear him.

Romans 6:23 – For the wages of sin is death

Revelation 20:13-15 – (13) And they were judged every man according to their works. (14) And death and hell were cast into the lake of fire ... (15) And whosoever was not found written in the book of life was cast into the lake of fire.

En'am 6:15 – Say: "I fear, if I rebel against my Lord, the retribution of an Awful Day.

Yunus 10:27 – As for those who have acquired evil deeds ... They are the owners of the Fire, dwelling in it forever.

104

Does a holy God take small sins seriously?

Bible **Yes** / **No** Qur'an

Matthew 5:19 – Whosoever, therefore, shall break one of these least commandments, and shall teach men so, he shall be called the least in the kingdom of heaven.

Matthew 12:36 – Every idle word that men shall speak, they shall give account thereof in the day of judgment.

John 8:34 – Jesus... verily I say unto you, Whosoever committeth sin is the servant of sin.

1 Corinthians 5:6 – Know ye not that a little leaven leaveneth the whole lump?

Galatians 3:10 – For as many as are of the works of the law are under the curse; for it is written, Cursed is everyone that continueth not in all things which are written in the book of the law, to do them...

James 2:10 – Whosoever shall ... offend in one point, he is guilty of all.

Ahzab 33:5 – And there is no sin for you in the mistakes that you make unintentionally but what your hearts purpose that will be a sin for you.

Nejm 53:31-32 – Those who avoid enormities of sin and abominations, and commit only small offences, for them your Lord is of vast mercy ... Therefore do not justify yourselves.

105

Is it a proper punishment to cut off the hands of a thief?

^{Bible} **No** / **Yes** ^{Qur'an}

Exodus 22:1-4, 9 – (1) If a man shall steal an ox, or a sheep, and kill it, or sell it, he shall restore five oxen of an ox, and four sheep for a sheep... (4) If the theft be certainly found in his hand alive, whether it be ox, or ass, or sheep, he shall restore double... (9) For all manner of trespass, whether it be for ox, for ass, for sheep, for raiment, or for any manner of lost thing, which another challengeth to be his, the cause of both parties shall come before the judges; and whom the judges shall condemn, he shall pay double unto his neighbor.

Proverbs 6:30-31 – (30) Men do not despise a thief, if he steal to satisfy his soul when he is hungry; (31) but if he be found, he shall restore.

Luke 6:35-36 – (35) But love ye your enemies, and do good, and lend, hoping for nothing again; and your reward shall be great ... (36) Be ye, therefore merciful as your Father also is merciful.

Maide 5:38 – As for the thief, both male and female, cut off their hands. It is the reward of their own deeds, and exemplary punishment from Allah.

106

Would it sometimes be ok for a believer to lie or deceive others in order to protect themselves? (Taqiyya or Kitman)

^{Bible} **No / Yes** ^{Qur'an}

Proverbs 6:16-17 – (16) These six things doth the Lord hate ... an abomination to him ... (17) a lying tongue.

Zephaniah 3:13 – The remnant of Israel shall not do iniquity, nor speak lies, neither shall a deceitful tongue be found in their mouth.

Ephesians 4:25 – Wherefore, put away lying, speak every man truth with his neighbour...

Revelation 21:8, 27 – (8) But the fearful, and unbelieving, and the abominable, and murderers, and whoremongers, and sorcerers, and idolaters, and all liars, shall have their part in the lake which burneth with fire and brimstone: which is the second death. (27) And there shall in no wise enter into it...

Bakara 2:225 – Allah will not call you to account for that which is unintentional in your oaths.

Tahrim 66:2 – Allah has made lawful for you (Muslims) absolution from your oaths.

* * * *

Note: Taqiyya means saying something that isn't true. Kitman is lying by omission.

107

Is homosexuality viewed as a sin which is forbidden and condemned?

^{Bible} **Yes** / **Yes** ^{Qur'an}

Leviticus 18:22 – Thou shalt not lie with mankind as with womankind: it is abomination.

Leviticus 20:13 – If a man also lie with mankind, as he lieth with a woman, both of them have committed an abomination: they shall surely be put to death; their blood shall be upon them.

1 Kings 14:24 – And there were also sodomites in the land; and they did according to all the abominations of the nations which the Lord cast out before the children of Israel.

Romans 1:26-27, 32 – (26) God gave them up unto vile affections ... (27) men with men working that which is unseemly; (32) they which commit such things are worthy of death.

A'raf 7:80-81 – (80) And Lot! (Remember) when he said to his people: "Will you commit foulness such as no creature ever did before you? (81) For you come with lust to men instead of women: you are indeed a people transgressing the bounds."

Neml 27:54-55 – (54) "Will you commit abomination knowingly? (55) Must you practice lust with men instead of women?"

108

Are abortion and murder viewed as sins which are forbidden and condemned?

^{Bible} **Yes / Yes** ^{Qur'an}

Genesis 9:6-7 – (6) Whoso sheddeth man's blood, by man shall his blood be shed; for in the image of God made he man. (7) And you, be ye fruitful, and multiply.

Exodus 20:13 – Thou shalt not kill.

Exodus 21:12 – He that smiteth a man, so that he die, shall be surely put to death.

Proverbs 6:16-17 – (16) These six things doth the Lord hate; yea seven are an abomination unto him ... (17) hands that shed innocent blood.

Amos 1:13 – Thus saith the LORD... I will not turn away their punishment, because they have ripped up the women with child...

Maide 5:32 – Whosoever kills a human being for other than manslaughter or corruption in the earth, it shall be as if he had killed all mankind.

En'am 6:151 – your Lord has made a sacred duty for you... that you slay not your children on a plea of want.

İsra 17:31 – Do not slay your offspring for fear of want. It is We who provide for them, and for you. Indeed their killing is a great sin.

109

Can the punishment for sin be erased by doing good works? (Sevap)

^{Bible} **No / Yes** ^{Qur'an}

Romans 3:28 – Therefore we conclude that a man is justified by faith without the deeds of the law.

Galatians 3:11 – But that no man is justified by the law in the sight of God, it is evident; for, The just shall live by faith.

Ephesians 2:8-9 – (8) For by grace are ye saved through faith; and that not of yourselves, it is the gift of God – (9) Not of works, lest any man should boast.

Titus 3:5-6 – (5) Not by works of righteousness which we have done, but according to his mercy.

James 2:10 – For whosoever shall keep the whole law, and yet offend in one point, he is guilty of all.

Hud 11:114 – Surely good deeds will annul evil ones.

Ankebut 29:7 – And as for those who believe and do good works, We shall remit from them their evil deeds and shall repay them the best that they did.

Nejm 53:32 – Those who avoid enormities of sin and abominations, and commit only small offences, for them your Lord is of vast mercy.

Salvation

110

Is a person born as a Christian or a Muslim?

^{Bible} **No / Yes** ^{Qur'an}

John 1:12-13 – (12) To become the sons of God, even to them that believe on his name; (13) Which were born, not of blood, nor of the will of the flesh, nor of the will of man, but of God.

John 3:5 – Jesus answered ... Except a man be born of water and of the Spirit, he cannot enter into the Kingdom of God.

1 Peter 1:23 – Being born again, not of corruptible seed, but of incorruptible, by the Word of God, which liveth and abideth forever.

Kâfirûn 109:1-6 – (1) Say: 'O disbelievers': (2) I do not worship what you worship, (3) Nor do you worship what I worship. (4) I shall never worship what you worship, (5) Nor will you ever worship what I worship. (6) To you belongs your religion, and to me mine.

* * * *

Note: According to the Bible one cannot be born a Christian; only those who are "born again" by the Spirit of God will inherit the kingdom of God. In Islam one who is born with a Muslim father is automatically considered to be a Muslim by birth.

111

Is a person's salvation contingent upon their own good works? (Ameller)

Bible **No / Yes** Qur'an

Romans 4:2-8 – (2) For if Abraham were justified by works, he hath something of which to glory, but not before God... (3) Abraham believed God, and it was counted unto him for righteousness. (4) Now to him that worketh is the reward not reckoned of grace, but of debt. (5) But to him that worketh not, but believeth on him that justifieth the ungodly, his faith is counted for righteousness... (6) God imputeth righteousness apart from works.

Ephesians 2:8-9 – (8) For by grace are ye saved through faith; and that not of yourselves, it is the gift of God: (9) Not of works, lest any man should boast.

Titus 3:5-6 – (5) Not by works of righteousness which we have done, but according to his mercy he saved us, by the washing of regeneration, and renewing of the Holy Ghost; (6) Which he shed on us abundantly through Jesus Christ our Saviour.

Hud 11:114 – Surely good deeds will annul evil ones.

Ankebut 29:7 – And as for those who believe and do good works, We shall remit from them their evil deeds and shall repay them the best that they did.

112

Is God's provision of salvation from the penalty of sin always dependent upon the ransom of a blood sacrifice? (Kefaret)

^{Bible} **Yes / No** ^{Qur'an}

Leviticus 17:11 – For the life of the flesh is in the blood; and I have given it to you upon the altar to make an atonement for your souls; for it is the blood that maketh atonement for the soul.

Matthew 20:28 – Even as the Son of man came not to be ministered unto, but to minister, and to give his life a ransom for many.

John 1:29 – John said, Behold the Lamb of God, which taketh away the sin of the world.

Hebrews 9:12, 22 – (12) By his own blood he ... obtained eternal redemption for us. (22) And almost all things are by the law purged with blood, and without shedding of blood is no remission.

Bakara 2:48 – And guard yourselves against a day when no soul shall aid another, and no intercession or ransom, or any compensation shall be accepted from it.

Hajj 22:37 – (Note it well that) neither their flesh nor their blood shall reach Allah. But it is your piety (and veneration) that reaches Him.

113

Can God's provision of salvation only be received by grace through faith in the sacrificial atonement of the Lamb of God? (Jesus Christ)

^{Bible} **Yes / No** ^{Qur'an}

John 1:29 – John ... saith, Behold the Lamb of God, which taketh away the sin of the world.

Romans 3:24-28 – (24) Being justified freely by his grace through the redemption that is in Christ Jesus: (25) Whom God hath set forth to be a propitiation through faith in his blood ... (28) Therefore we conclude that a man is justified by faith without the deeds of the law.

Ephesians 1:7 – We have redemption through his blood, the forgiveness of sins, according to the riches of his grace.

Ephesians 2:8 – By grace are ye saved through faith.

Titus 3:5-6 – (5) Not by works of righteousness which we have done, but according to his mercy he saved us, by the washing of regeneration, and renewing of the Holy Ghost, (6) Which he shed on us abundantly through Jesus Christ, our Saviour.

En'am 6:164 – Each soul earns only on its own account, nor do any laden bear another's load.

İsra 17:15 – No soul can bear another's burden.

Nejm 53:38 – No soul shall bear another's burden.

114

In order for a person to obtain eternal life is it first necessary for them to hear and understand the Gospel of Jesus Christ and believe that God sent Him to be the Messiah, the Savior of the world?

^{Bible} **Yes** / **No** ^{Qur'an}

Romans 10:8-17 – (8) the word of faith, which we preach: (9) That if thou shalt confess with thy mouth the Lord Jesus, and shalt believe in thine heart that God raised him from the dead, thou shalt be saved. (10) For with the heart man believeth unto righteousness; and with the mouth confession is made unto salvation... (13) For whosoever shall call upon the name of the Lord shall be saved. (14) How then shall they call on him in whom they have not believed? And how shall they believe in him of whom they have not heard? And how shall they hear without a preacher? (15) And how shall they preach, except they be sent?... (17) So, then, faith cometh by hearing, and hearing by the word of God.

Bakara 2:119-120 – (119) We have sent you (O Muhammad) with the truth, and as a bringer of glad tidings and a warning ... (120) Neither Christians nor the Jews will be pleased with you until you follow their faith. Say, "the guidance of Allah is the (only) guidance."

115

Is it accepted that belief in Jesus Christ as Savior and Lord is the only way for a person's sins to be forgiven and to obtain eternal life?

^{Bible} **Yes** / **No** ^{Qur'an}

John 3:16, 36 – (16) For God so loved the world, that he gave his only begotten Son, that whosoever believeth in him should not perish, but have everlasting life... (36) He that believeth on the Son hath everlasting life; and he that believeth not the Son of God shall not see life, but the wrath of God abideth on him.

John 14:6 – Jesus saith ... I am the way, the truth, and the life; no man cometh unto the Father, but by me.

John 17:3 – And this is life eternal, that they might know thee, the only true God, and Jesus Christ, whom thou hast sent.

Acts 4:10-12 – (10) By the name of Jesus Christ of Nazareth, whom ye crucified, whom God raised from the dead... (12) Neither is there salvation in any other: for there is none other name under heaven given among men, whereby we must be saved.

Al-i İmran 3:19-20 – (19) The true religion in the sight of Allah is Islam. Those who formerly received the Scripture disagreed among themselves through jealousy only after knowledge came to them ... (20) If they become Muslims they shall be rightly guided; if they turn away, then your duty is only to inform them.

116

Is water baptism required of a believer today?

^{Bible} **Yes / No** ^{Qur'an}

Matthew 28:18-20 – (18) Jesus came and spake ... All power is given unto me in heaven and in earth. (19) Go ye, therefore, and teach all nations, baptizing them in the name of the Father, and of the Son, and the Holy Ghost, (20) Teaching them to observe all things whatsoever I have commanded you; and lo, I am with you always, even unto the end of the world.

Mark 16:15-16 – (15) And he said unto them, Go ye into all the world and preach the gospel to every creature. (16) He that believeth and is baptized shall be saved; but he that believeth not shall be damned.

Acts 2:38 – Then Peter said unto them, Repent and be baptized, every one of you, in the name of Jesus Christ for the remission of sins, and ye shall receive the gift of the Holy Ghost.

Acts 22:16 – And now why tarriest thou? Arise and be baptized and wash away thy sins, calling on the name of the Lord.

* * * *

Note: There are no verses in the Qur'an which talk about water baptism.

117

Is circumcision required of a male believer today?

^{Bible} **No / Yes** ^{Qur'an}

Acts 15:5-11 – (5) But there rose up certain of the sect of the Pharisees, which believed, saying that it was needful to circumcise them, and to keep the law of Moses… (7) Peter rose up and said unto them.… (10) Why tempt ye God, to put a yoke upon the neck of the disciples, which neither our fathers nor we were able to bear?

1 Corinthians 7:18, 20 – (18) Is any man called being circumcised? Let him not become uncircumcised. Is any called in uncircumcision? Let him not be circumcised … (20) Let every man abide in the same calling wherein he was called.

Galatians 5:2 – I, Paul, say unto you, that if ye be circumcised, Christ shall profit you nothing.

Galatians 5:6 – For in Jesus Christ neither circumcision availeth anything, nor uncircumcision, but faith which worketh by love.

Nahl 16:123 – We revealed to you (O Muhammad) saying: "Follow the religion of Abraham."

* * * *

Note: In Islam, circumcision is part of the religion of Abraham, and is thus considered as binding on Muslims. This is also seen in the Hadith: Bukhari 1252, Fatih al-Bari 6:388; and Muslim 4:2370.

118

Are there verses which command people to be holy, and is holiness a pre-requisite for entering into heaven?

^{Bible} **Yes** / **No** ^{Qur'an}

Leviticus 11:44 – For I am the LORD your God: ye shall therefore sanctify yourselves, and ye shall be holy; for I am holy.

1 Corinthians 3:16-17 – (16) Know ye not that ye are the temple of God, and that the Spirit of God dwelleth in you? (17) If any man defile the temple of God, him shall God destroy; for the temple of God is holy, which temple ye are.

1 Thessalonians 3.13 – he may establish your hearts unblamable in holiness before God.

1 Thessalonians 4:7 – For God hath not called us unto uncleanness, but unto holiness.

Hebrews 12:14 – Follow peace with all men, and holiness, without which no man shall see the Lord.

1 Peter 1:15-16 – (15) But, as he which hath called you is holy, so be ye holy in all manner of conversation, (16) Because it is written, Be ye holy; for I am holy.

Revelation 22:11 – And he that is holy, let him be holy still.

* * * *

Note: There are no verses in the Qur'an which command people to be holy or indicate that they can be holy.

119

Can people choose to become the children of God through an exercise of their own free will and volition?

_{Bible} **Yes / No** _{Qur'an}

John 1:12 – But as many as received him, to them gave he power to become the sons of God.

Romans 8:14, 16 – (14) For as many as are led by the Spirit of God, they are the sons of God ... (16) The Spirit itself beareth witness with our spirit, that we are the children of God.

Galatians 3:26 – For ye are all the children of God by faith in Christ Jesus.

Galatians 4:6-7 – (6) And because ye are sons, God hath sent forth the Spirit of his Son into your hearts, crying Abba, Father. (7) Wherefore, thou art no more a servant, but a son; and if a son, then an heir of God through Christ.

Hebrews 12:5-6 – (5) The exhortation ... as children. My son, despise not thou the chastening of the Lord ... (6) For whom the Lord loveth he chasteneth.

Revelation 3:20 – if any man hear my voice and open the door, I will come in to him...

Maide 5:18 – The Jews and the Christians say: "We are the sons of Allah, and His loved ones." Say: "Why then does He chastise you for your sins? Surely you are but mortals of His creating."

120

Is a person's fate totally predetermined or predestined by God? (Kader or Kısmet)

^{Bible} **No** / **Yes** ^{Qur'an}

Deuteronomy 11:26-27 – (26) Behold, I set before you this day a blessing and a curse. (27) A blessing if ye obey the commandments.

Deuteronomy 30:19 – I have set before you life and death, blessing and cursing; therefore, choose life.

Joshua 24:15 – Choose you this day whom ye will serve ... but as for me and my house, we will serve the LORD.

Tevbe 9:51 – Say: "Nothing will befall us except what Allah has ordained."

Kasas 28:68 – They have never any choice.

Ahzab 33:36, 38 – (33) And it is not for a believing man or woman to have any choice in their affairs when Allah and His messenger have decided an affair for them... (38) ...the commandment of Allah is certain destiny.

* * * *

Note: Among Christians, Arminians would say no; but Calvinists would say yes.

121

Does God use a scale of balances to measure a person's good and bad works to determine whether they will go to heaven or to hell? (Terazi)

^{Bible} **No / Yes** ^{Qur'an}

Romans 3:20 – Therefore, by the deeds of the law there shall no flesh be justified in his sight; for by the law is the knowledge of sin.

Ephesians 2:8-9 – (8) For by grace are ye saved through faith; and that not of yourselves, it is the gift of God (9) Not of works, lest any man should boast.

2 Timothy 1:9 – Who hath saved us, and called us with an holy calling, not according to our works, but according to his own purpose and grace, which was given us in Christ Jesus before the world began.

Titus 3:4-5 – (4) But after the kindness and love of God, our Saviour toward man appeared, (5) Not by works of righteousness which we have done, but according to his mercy he saved us.

A'raf 7:8-9 – (8) As for those whose scale is heavy, they are the successful. (9) And as for those whose scale is light: those are they who lose their souls.

Mü'minun 23:102-103 – (102) Then those whose scales are heavy, they are successful. (103) And those whose scales are light have lost themselves, they shall abide in hell forever.

122

In order for a person to be able to enter into the kingdom of God, is it first necessary to have a spiritual rebirth and be "born again"?

^{Bible} **Yes** / **No** ^{Qur'an}

John 1:12-13 – (12) But as many as received him, to them gave he power to become the sons of God, even to them that believe on his name; (13) Which were born, not of blood, nor of the will of the flesh, nor of the will of man, but of God.

John 3:3 – Jesus answered ... Except a man be born again, he cannot see the kingdom of God.

2 Corinthians 5:17 – Therefore, if any man be in Christ, he is a new creature; old things are passed away; behold, all things are become new.

1 Peter 1:23 – Being born again, not of corruptible seed, but of incorruptible, by the word of God, which liveth and abideth forever.

1 John 2:29 – If ye know that... everyone that doeth righteousness is born of him.

1 John 4:7 – everyone that loveth is born of God, and knoweth God.

* * * *

Note: The Qur'an does not mention anything about the need for a spiritual rebirth or being "born again."

123

Does God give the promise or guarantee of eternal life to all true believers in Christ?

^{Bible} **Yes** / **Yes** ^{Qur'an}

John 3:16 – For God so loved the world, that he gave his only begotten Son, that whosoever believeth in him should not perish, but have everlasting life.

John 3:36 – He that believeth on the Son hath everlasting life.

John 5:24 – He that heareth my word, and believeth on him that sent me, hath everlasting life.

John 10:28 – And I will give unto them eternal life; and they shall never perish, neither shall any man pluck them out of my hand.

1 John 5:11 – And this is the record, that God hath given to us eternal life, and this life is in his Son.

Al-i İmran 3:55, 113-115 – (55) Allah said: "O Jesus! I am ... setting those who follow you above those who disbelieve until the Day of Resurrection. (113) Among the People of the Scripture there is an upright community ... (114) They are of the righteous. (115) And whatever good they do, its reward will not be denied them.

Maide 5:47, 69 – (47) The People of the Gospel ... those who believe ... (69) Who are Christians, whoso believes in Allah and the last Day and does right, no fear come upon them.

Future Things

124

Are the words "prophet" and "prophecy" used primarily in reference to a person who by the gift of God has knowledge of future things? (Nebi)

^{Bible} <u>Yes</u> / <u>No</u> ^{Qur'an}

1 Samuel 9:9 – Beforetime in Israel, when a man went to enquire of God, thus he spake, Come, and let us go to the seer; for he that is now called a Prophet was beforetime called a Seer.

Mark 13:23 – behold, I have foretold you all things.

John 16:13 – When he, the Spirit of Truth, is come… he will shew you things to come.

Acts 3:18 – But those things, which God before had shewed by the mouth of all his prophets, that Christ should suffer, he hath so fulfilled.

Revelation 19:10 – The testimony of Jesus is the spirit of prophecy.

A'raf 7:158, 188 – (158) So believe in Allah and His messenger, the prophet who can neither read nor write. (188) I am but a warner, and a bearer of glad tidings unto people who believe.

Ahkaf 46:9 – Say to them: "I am no new thing among the Messengers. Just as all the former Prophets were mortals who had no share in Divine attributes and powers, so am I. I am no more than a plain warner.

125

Is detailed information given concerning future events at the end of the world? (Eschatology / Gayb Haber)

^{Bible} **Yes** / **No** ^{Qur'an}

Matthew 24:3, 14, 25 – (3) Tell us, when shall these things be? And what shall be the sign of thy coming, and of the end of the world? (14) And this gospel of the kingdom shall be preached in all the world for a witness unto all nations; and then shall the end come. (25) Behold, I have told you before.

Revelation 1:1 – The Revelation of Jesus Christ, which God gave unto him, to shew unto his servants things which must shortly come to pass.

En'am 6:50 – Say of Muhammad, to the disbelievers: "I say not to you that I possess the treasures of Allah, nor that I have knowledge of the Unseen; and I say not to you; "I am an angel." I follow only that which is inspired in me."

Ahkaf 46:9 – Say to them: "I am no new thing among the Messengers. I do not know what shall befall you tomorrow or what shall befall me. I only follow that which is revealed to me, and I am no more than a plain warner."

126

Are there prophetic verses predicting the coming of a powerful satanic world ruler who will come in the last days? (Antichrist / Mehdi)

^{Bible} **Yes** / **No** ^{Qur'an}

Matthew 24:21-25 – (23) Believe it not. (24) For there shall arise false Christs, and false prophets.

2 Thessalonians 2:7-9 – (8) And then shall that Wicked be revealed, whom the Lord shall consume with the spirit of his mouth ... (9) even him whose coming is after the working of Satan.

1 John 2:18 – Little children, it is the last time; and as ye have heard that antichrist shall come, even now are there many antichrists, whereby we know that it is the last time.

Revelation 6:1-2 – (2) And I saw, and behold a white horse; and he that sat on him had a bow; and a crown was given to him, and he went forth conquering, and to conquer.

Revelation 13:1-7 – (4) Who is like unto the beast? Who is able to make war with him?... (7) And it was given unto him to make war with the saints, and to overcome them...

* * * *

Note: The Qur'an does not mention the coming of the Antichrist or the Mehdi.

127

Will there be a day of judgment when God will raise each and every person from the dead and judge whether they will go to heaven or to hell? (Ahiret Günü)

^{Bible} **Yes / Yes** ^{Qur'an}

Psalm 96:12-13 – (12) Rejoice before the Lord; for he cometh to judge the earth; (13) he shall judge the world with righteousness, and the peoples with his truth.

Hebrews 9:27 – And as it is appointed unto men once to die, but after this the judgment.

2 Peter 2:9 – The Lord knoweth how to deliver the godly out of temptations, and to reserve the unjust unto the day of judgment to be punished.

Revelation 20:11-15 – (12) And the dead were judged ... (15) And whosoever was not found written in the book of life was cast into the lake of fire.

Bakara 2:113 – Allah will judge between them on the Day of Resurrection concerning wherein they differ.

Nisa 4:87 – Allah! There is no God save Him. He gathers you all to a Day of Resurrection about which there is no doubt.

Al-i İmran 3:185 – Every soul shall taste of death. And you shall be paid on the Day of Resurrection only that which you have fairly earned.

128

Will everyone have to spend a period of time suffering in hell?

^{Bible} **No / <u>Yes</u>** ^{Qur'an}

John 5:24 – He that heareth my word, and believeth on him that sent me, hath everlasting life, and shall not come into condemnation, but is passed from death unto life.

Romans 8:1-2 – (1) There is therefore, now no condemnation to them which are in Christ Jesus… (2) For the law of the spirit of life in Christ Jesus hath made me free from the law of sin and death.

1 Thessalonians 5:9 – God hath not appointed us to wrath but to obtain salvation by our Lord Jesus Christ.

Al-i İmran 3:185 – Whoever is removed from the fire of Hell and is made to enter the Garden.

Meryem 19:70-72 – (70) And certainly We know best who deserves to be burnt there. (71) There is not one of you who shall not come to it. This is the absolute decree of your Lord. (72) Then We shall rescue those who kept from evil and leave the evil-doers therein crouching.

Sejde 32:13 – And if We had so willed, We could have given every soul its guidance, but the word from Me concerning evil doers took effect: that I will fill hell with the jinn and mankind together.

129

If a person goes to hell, is there ever a possibility of getting out later on and going to heaven?

_{Bible} **No** / **Yes** ^{Qur'an}

Matthew 25:41, 46 – (41) Then shall he say also unto them on the left hand, Depart from me, ye cursed, into everlasting fire, prepared for the devil and his angels ... (46) And these shall go away into everlasting punishment.

Luke 16:25-26 – (25) Abraham said ... now he is comforted, and thou art tormented. (26) Between us and you there is a great gulf fixed, so that they which would pass from hence to you cannot; neither can they pass to us, that would come from thence.

En'am 6:128 – He will say: "Fire is your home. Dwell therein forever, except him whom Allah wills to deliver.

Hud 11:106-107 – (106) As for the wretched, they shall be in the Fire ... (107) Eternally therein ... unless your Lord ordains otherwise.

Meryem 19:70-72 – (70) We know best who deserves most to be burnt there. (71) There is not one of you who shall not come to it. This is the absolute decree of your Lord. (72) Then We shall rescue those who kept from evil and leave the evil doers therein crouching.

* * * *

Note: Muhammad was uncertain about whether he himself would end up going to heaven (Bukhari 5:266)

130

Is the resurrection body a physical body of flesh, bone and blood?

^{Bible} **No / Yes** ^{Qur'an}

1 Corinthians 15:35-50 – (35) But some man will say, How are the dead raised up? And with what body do they come? (36) Thou fool... (40) There are also celestial bodies, and bodies terrestrial; but the glory of the celestial is one, and the glory of the terrestrial is another... (42) So also is the resurrection of the dead... (44) It is sown a natural body, it is raised a spiritual body. There is a natural body and there is a spiritual body... (50) Now this I say, brethren, that flesh and blood cannot inherit the kingdom of God...

Bakara 2:25, 259 – (25) There will be pure spouses for them, and they will abide there forever. (259) See how We will raise them and clothe them with flesh.

Zukhruf 43:70 – Enter the Garden, you and your wives, to be made glad.

Tur 52:20 – And We shall wed them to houris with large and lovely eyes.

Vakia 56:35-38 – (35) We created the women again, (36) and made them virgins, loving companions of the same age.

Nebe 78:33 – Youthful maidens of equal age with firm breasts.

131

Will there be sexual relationships and marriage in heaven? (Houris)

^{Bible} **No / Yes** ^{Qur'an}

Matthew 22:28-33 – (28) In the resurrection whose wife shall she be? ... for they all had her. (29) Jesus answered ... Ye do err, not knowing the scriptures, nor the power of God. (30) For in the resurrection they neither marry, nor are given in marriage, but are as the angels of God in heaven.

1 Corinthians 15:50 – Flesh and blood cannot enter the kingdom of God; neither doth corruption inherit incorruption.

Bakara 2:25, 259 – (25) There will be pure spouses for them, and they will abide there forever... (259) See how We will raise them and clothe them with flesh.

Zuhruf 43:70 – ...Enter the Garden, you and your wives, to be made glad.

Tur 52:20 – And We shall wed them to houris with large and lovely eyes.

Vakia 56:22, 35-37 – (22) fair ones with wide, lovely eyes... (35) We created the women again, 36. And made them virgins, (37) Loving companions of the same age.

Nebe 78:33 – Youthful maidens of equal age with firm breasts.

132

Is the universal church considered to be the "Bride of Christ"?

^{Bible} **Yes** / **No** ^{Qur'an}

Romans 7:4 – Wherefore, my brethren, ye also are become dead to the law by the body of Christ; that ye should be married to another, [even] to him who is raised from the dead, that we should bring forth fruit unto God.

Ephesians 5:23, 25, 32 – (23) Christ is the head of the church ... (25) Husbands, love your wives, even as Christ also loved the church, and gave himself for it ... (32) This is a great mystery, but I speak concerning Christ and the church.

Revelation 19:7 – Let us be glad and rejoice, and give honour to him: for the marriage of the Lamb is come, and his wife hath made herself ready.

Revelation 21:9 – Come hither, I will shew thee the bride, the Lamb's wife.

Revelation 22:17 – And the Spirit and the bride say, Come. And let him that heareth say, Come. And let him that is athirst come. And whosoever will, let him take the water of life freely.

* * * *

Note: The Qur'an only mentions the church once and does not mention the "Bride of Christ": Hajj 22:40.

Practical Life Issues

133

Does God want believers today to live under the law? (Shariah)

^{Bible} **No** / **Yes** ^{Qur'an}

Romans 3:20, 28 – (20) Therefore by the deeds of the law there shall no flesh be justified in his sight; for by the law is the knowledge of sin... (28) Therefore we conclude that man is justified by faith apart from the deeds of the law.

Romans 6:14 – For sin shall not have dominion over you; for ye are not under the law but under grace.

Romans 10:4 – For Christ is the end of the law for righteousness to everyone that believeth.

Galatians 3:11, 25 – (11) But that no man is justified by the law in the sight of God, it is evident; for, The just shall live by faith. (25) But after faith is come, we are no longer under a schoolmaster.

Maide 5:48 – We have appointed a (divine) law and a traced-out way.

Jathiyah 45:18 – And now We have set you (O Muhammad) on a clear road of (Our) commandment; so follow it.

134

Is it forbidden for a believer to drink wine?

^{Bible} **No / Yes** ^{Qur'an}

Genesis 27:21-28 – (21) And Isaac said unto Jacob, Come near… (25) he brought him wine, and he drank. (28) God give thee of the dew of heaven, and the fatness of the earth, and plenty of corn and wine.

Numbers 6:20 – And the priest shall wave them for a wave offering before the LORD… and after that the Nazarite may drink wine.

Luke 7:34-35 – (34) The Son of man is come eating and drinking; and ye say, Behold, a gluttonous man, and a winebibber, a friend of publicans and sinners! (35) But wisdom is justified of all her children.

John 2:1-11 – (3) They wanted wine … (7) Jesus saith … Fill the waterpots with water … (9) that was made wine.

1 Timothy 5:23 – Drink no longer water, but use a little wine for thy stomach's sake and thy frequent infirmities.

Bakara 2:219 – They ask you about drinking and gambling. Say: "There is great harm in both."

Maide 5:90-91 – (90) O you who believe! Intoxicants and gambling, and (occult dedication of) stones and divining arrows are only an infamy of Satan's handiwork. Leave them aside in order that you may succeed. (91) Will you not then abstain?

135

Is it forbidden for a believer to eat pork?

Bible **No / Yes** Qur'an

Acts 10:13-15 – (13) Rise, Peter; kill and eat. (14) But Peter said, Not so, Lord; for I have never eaten anything that is common or unclean. (15) And the voice spake unto him the second time, What God hath cleansed, that call not thou common.

Romans 14:14 – I know and am persuaded by the Lord Jesus, that there is nothing unclean of itself; but to him that esteemeth anything to be unclean, to him it is unclean.

1 Corinthians 6:12 – All things are lawful unto me, but all things are not expedient; all things are lawful for me, but I will not be brought under the power of any.

1 Corinthians 10:25 – Whatsoever is sold in the shambles, that eat, asking no question for conscience sake.

Colossians 2:16 – Let no man therefore judge you in meat, or in drink.

Maide 5:3 – Forbidden to you (for food) are carrion and blood and swineflesh.

En'am 6:145 – Say: "(of meat) prohibited to an eater that he eat thereof ... be carrion, or blood poured forth, or swineflesh, for that assuredly is foul."

Nahl 16:115 – He has forbidden you only carrion, blood and the flesh of swine...

136

Does God expect believers to fast today?

Bible **Yes** / **Yes** Qur'an

Joel 2:12 – Therefore also now, saith the LORD, turn ye *even* to me with all your heart, and with fasting, and with weeping, and with mourning.

Matthew 6:17-18 – (17) But thou, when thou fastest, anoint thine head, and wash thy face; (18) That thou appear not unto men to fast, but unto thy Father which is in secret: and thy Father, which seeth in secret, shall reward thee openly.

Mark 2:20 – But the days will come, when the bridegroom shall be taken away from them, and then shall they fast in those days.

1 Corinthians 7:5 – Give yourselves to fasting and prayer; and come together again.

Bakara 2:183, 185 – (183) O you who believe! Fasting is prescribed for you, as it was prescribed for those who came before you ... (185) The month of Ramadan in which the Qur'an was revealed ... whoever of you is present in that month let him fast.

Ahzab 33:35 – Behold; men who surrender to Allah ... men who fast and women who fast ... Allah has prepared for them forgiveness, and a vast reward.

* * * *

Note: Fasting is mentioned 46 times in the Bible, and 20 times in the Qur'an.

137

Does God prefer that prayer and fasting be done openly where you can be seen by others?

^{Bible} **No** / **Yes** ^{Qur'an}

Matthew 6:5-8 – (6) But thou, when thou prayest, enter into thy closet, and when thou hast shut thy door, pray to thy Father which is in secret; and thy Father which seeth in secret shall reward thee openly.

Matthew 6:16-18 – (16) Moreover, when ye fast, be not, as the hypocrites, of a sad countenance; for they disfigure their faces, that they may appear unto men to fast. Verily I say unto you, They have their reward. (17) But thou, when thou fastest, anoint thine head, and wash thy face, (18) That thou appear not unto men to fast, but unto thy Father, who seeth in secret; and thy Father who seeth in secret, shall reward thee openly.

Nisa 4:103 – And when you have performed (congregational) prayers, then remember Allah standing, sitting and reclining.

Jumah 62:9 – O believers! When a call is heard for the prayer of the day of congregation, hasten to the remembrance of Allah and cease your trading. That is better for you if you but knew it.

* * * *

Note: Bukhari's Hadith 11:620: Narrated Abu Huraira: Allah's Apostle said, "The reward of the prayer offered by a person in congregation is twenty five times greater than that of the prayer offered in one's house or in the market (alone).

138

Does God want people to fast during the day and feast at night for one month out of every year? (Ramadan)

^{Bible} **No** / **Yes** ^{Qur'an}

Isaiah 58:3-7 – (6) Is not this the fast that I have chosen? to loose the bands of wickedness, to undo the heavy burdens, and to let the oppressed go free, and that ye break every yoke?

Matthew 6:16-18 – (16) Moreover, when ye fast, be not, as the hypocrites, of a sad countenance; for they disfigure their faces, that they may appear unto men to fast. Verily I say unto you, They have their reward. (17) But thou, when thou fastest, anoint thine head, and wash thy face, (18) That thou appear not unto men to fast, but unto the Father, who is in secret; and thy Father, who seeth in secret, shall reward thee openly.

Bakara 2:183-185 – (183) O you who believe! Fasting is prescribed for you, as it was prescribed for those who came before you... (184) (Fast) a certain number of days, but if any one of you is ill or on a journey, let him (break his fast, and) fast the same number days later on... (185) The month of Ramadan in which the Qur'an was revealed, a guidance for mankind, (a book of) clear proofs of guidance and the criterion (distinguishing right from wrong). Therefore whoever of you is present in that month let him fast; but he who is ill or on a journey shall fast (a same) number of days later on. Allah desires for your ease.

139

Does God expect believers to tithe and give alms? (Zekat)

^{Bible} **Yes** / **Yes** ^{Qur'an}

Malachi 3:8 – Will a man rob God? Yet ye have robbed me. But ye say, Wherein have we robbed thee? In tithes and offerings.

Matthew 6:3 – But when thou doest alms, let not thy left hand know what thy right hand doeth.

Luke 6:30 – Give to every man that asketh of thee...

Luke 12:33 – Sell what ye have and give alms.

Matthew 19:21 – Go and sell what thou hast, and give to the poor, and thou shalt have treasure in heaven; and come and follow me.

Luke 11:41 – Give alms of such things as ye have.

Acts 20:35 – Ye ought to support the weak... it is more blessed to give than to receive.

Ephesians 4:28 – Give to him that needeth.

Bakara 2:177 – Establish the prayer and pay the zakat.

Tevbe 9:103-104 – (103) Take alms of their wealth ... (104) Allah ... receives (approves of) their alms.

Mu'minun 23:1, 4 – (1) Successful indeed are the believers ... (4) and those who are payers of the Zakat.

140

Does God want to listen to ritual prayers said over and over again five times a day at the same time every day? (Namaz)

^{Bible} **No / Yes** ^{Qur'an}

Matthew 6:5-8 – (5) And when thou prayest, thou shalt not be as the hypocrites are; for they love to pray standing in the synagogues and at the corners of the streets, that they may be seen of men. Verily I say unto you. They have their reward. (6) But thou, when thou prayest, enter into thy room, and when thou hast shut thy door, pray to thy Father, who is in secret; and thy Father, who seeth in secret, shall reward thee openly. (7) But when ye pray, use not vain repetitions, as the pagans do; for they think that they shall be heard for their much speaking. Be not ye, therefore, like unto them; for your Father knoweth what things ye have need of, before ye ask him. (8) Be not ye therefore like unto them; for your Father knoweth what things ye have...

John 4:24 – God is a Spirit; and they that worship him must worship him in spirit and in truth.

Bakara 2:45 – Seek help in patience and with Salat.

Hud 11:114 – And establish the Prayer at the two ends of the day and at the approaches of the night.

İsra 17:78 – Establish the Prayer at the sun's decline until the darkness of the night; and the recital of veil dawn, for the recital (in the prayer) at dawn has its witness.

141

Does God expect believers to make a pilgrimage to a holy place at least once in their lifetime? (Hajj)

^{Bible} **No** / **Yes** ^{Qur'an}

Matthew 24:24-26 – (26) If they shall say unto you, Behold, he is in the desert; go not forth.

John 4:19-24 – (19) The woman saith unto him, Sir, I perceive that thou art a prophet. (20) Our fathers worshipped in this mountain; and ye say that in Jerusalem is the place where men ought to worship. (21) Jesus saith unto her, Woman, believe me, the hour cometh, when ye shall neither in this mountain, nor yet at Jerusalem, worship the Father. (22) Ye worship ye know not what. We know what we worship; for salvation is of the Jews. (23) But the hour cometh, and now is, when the true worshippers shall worship the Father in spirit and in truth; for the Father seeketh such to worship him. (24) God is a Spirit; and they that worship him must worship him in spirit and in truth.

Bakara 2:196 – Perform the Greater and the Lesser Pilgrimage (Hajj and 'Umra) for Allah.

Al-i İmran 3:97 – And pilgrimage to the House is a duty to Allah for mankind, for all who are able to make the journey.

Hajj 22:26-31 – (27) And proclaim among the people the pilgrimage!... (31) (Perform your duties of Hajj) being men of pure faith...

142

Does God still want people today to offer animal sacrifices once a year? (Kurban)

^{Bible} **No / Yes** ^{Qur'an}

Psalm 51:16-17 – (16) For thou desirest not sacrifice, else would I give it; thou delightest not in burnt offering. (17) The sacrifices of God are a broken spirit; a broken and a contrite heart, O God, thou wilt not despise.

Hebrews 9:11-12, 25-28 – (11) But Christ ... (12) by his own blood he entered in once into the holy place, having obtained eternal redemption for us ... (25) Nor yet that he should offer himself often ... (26) but now once in the end of the world hath he appeared to put away sin by the sacrifice of himself ... (28) So Christ was once offered to bear the sins of many.

Bakara 2:196 – Whoever is ill or has an ailment of the head must pay a ransom, either by fasting or by almsgiving, or by offering a sacrifice.

Hajj 22:28, 34 – (28) Mention the name of Allah, over the beasts of cattle He has provided them. Then eat thereof, and feed the unfortunate and distressed poor. (34) And for every nation We have appointed a ritual for sacrifice.

143

If a Muslim has a question about something in the Bible, would it be appropriate for him to ask a Christian or a Jew about it?

Bible **Yes** / **Yes** Qur'an

Acts 17:10-11 – (10) And the brethren immediately sent away Paul and Silas by night unto Berea: who coming thither went into the synagogue of the Jews. (11) These were more noble than those in Thessalonica, in that they received the word with all readiness of mind, and searched the scriptures daily, whether those things were so.

1 Peter 3:15 – But sanctify the Lord God in your hearts: and be ready always to give an answer to every man that asketh you a reason of the hope that is in you with meekness and fear.

Yunus 10:94 – If you are in doubt regarding what We have revealed to you, then ask those who have been reading the Book before you. The truth has come to you from your Lord, therefore do not doubt it.

Nahl 16:43 – The messengers We sent before you (O Muhammad)... We gave revelation. Ask the people of the Remembrance if you do not know.

Enbiya 21:7 – Before you (also), the messengers We sent were only men, to whom We had granted revelation. If you do not know this, ask those who have the Reminder.

144

If a person has reservations about something in one of the Holy Books, should the believer avoid asking honest questions if he might not like the answers?

_{Bible} **No / Yes** _{Qur'an}

Acts 17:11 – These were more noble than those in Thessalonica, in that they received the word with all readiness of mind, and searched the scriptures daily, whether those things were so.

1 John 4:1 – Beloved, believe not every spirit, but try the spirits whether they are of God: because many false prophets are gone out into the world.

Bakara 2:108 – Or would you then question your Prophet as Moses was once questioned? He who changes belief for disbelief surely strays from the right path.

Maide 5:101-102 – (101) O you who believe! Ask not of things which, if they were made known to you, would trouble you; but if you ask of them when the Qur'an is being revealed, they will be made known to you. (102) A people before you asked, and then disbelieved therein.

Ahzab 33:36 – And it is not for a believing man or a believing woman to have any choice in their affairs when Allah and His Messenger have decided an affair for them.

145

Aside from divine revelation, are the traditional sayings and interpretations of men considered to be trustworthy and needed to properly understand the Holy Books? (Sola Scriptura / Hadith)

^{Bible} **No / Yes** ^{Qur'an}

Jeremiah 7:8 – Behold, ye trust in lying words that cannot profit...

Romans 3:4 – God forbid: yea, let God be true, but every man a liar; as it is written, That thou mightest be justified in thy sayings, and mightest overcome when thou art judged.

Nejm 52:33-34 – (33) Do they say: "He has invented it (the Qur'an) himself?" ... (34) Let them produce a speech like it, if what they say be true.

* * * *

Note: Within Islam the most trusted and frequently used collectors of the Hadith include Ibn Ishaq (d. 768); Ebu Davud (d. 775); Ibn Hisham (d. 833); Muhammad al-Bukhari (d. 870); Sahih Muslim (d. 875); İbn Maje (d. 886); al-Tirmidhi (d. 892); Ebu Jafer Taberi (d. 923); None of these men lived during or even close to Muhammad's lifetime (570-632). Out of 600,000 hadith Bukhari collected during 16 years, he only kept 7,397 as being genuine (sahih). He threw away over 99% of what he collected from religious Muslims as being exaggerated or untrue.

146

Does God expect believers to actively worship together and propagate their faith today?

^{Bible} **Yes / Yes** ^{Qur'an}

Isaiah 6:8 – Also I heard the voice of the Lord, saying, Whom shall I send, and who will go for us? Then I said, Here am I; send me.

Matthew 28:19 – Go ye, therefore, and teach all nations, baptizing them in the name of the Father, and of the Son, and of the Holy Ghost.

Acts 4:18-20 – (18) And they called them, and commanded them not to speak at all nor teach in the name of Jesus... (20) we cannot but speak the things which we have seen and heard.

2 Corinthians 5:20 – We are ambassadors of Christ, as though God did beseech you by us.

1 Peter 3:15 – Be ready always to give an answer to every man that asketh you a reason of the hope that is in you with meekness and fear.

Tevbe 9:33 – It is He who has sent His messenger with the guidance and the religion of truth to make it triumphant above all religion.

Nahl 16:125 – Invite (all) to the path of your Lord with wisdom and kindly exhortation, and reason with them.

147

Does God want believers to break up into various sects, denominations and splinter groups?

^{Bible} **No / No** ^{Qur'an}

John 17:20-21 – (20) Neither pray I for these alone, but for them also which shall believe on me through their word; (21) That they may be one, as thou, Father, art in me, and I in thee, that they also may be one in us; that the world may believe that thou hast sent me.

1 Corinthians 1:10 – Now I beseech you, brethren, by the name of our Lord Jesus Christ, that ye all speak the same thing, and that there be no divisions among you, but that ye be perfectly joined together in the same mind and in the same judgment.

1 Corinthians 3:3-4 – (3) For ye are yet carnal; for whereas there is among you envying, and strife, and divisions, are ye not carnal, and walk as men? (4) For while one saith, I am of Paul; and another, I am of Apollos; are ye not carnal?

Al-i İmran 3:103 – And hold fast, all together, to the rope of Allah, and do not separate.

En'am 6:159 – As for those who divide their religion and become divided into different sects, no concern at all have you with them. Their case will go to Allah who will tell them what they used to do.

148

Are there verses in the Holy Books which encourage people to be joyful and happy here in this life on earth?

^{Bible} **Yes** / **No** ^{Qur'an}

Deuteronomy 12:12, 18 – (12) ye shall rejoice before the LORD your God, ye, and your sons, and your daughters... (18) thou shall rejoice before the Lord your God in all that thou putteth thine hands unto.

Psalm 5:11 – But let all those who put their trust in thee rejoice; let them ever shout for joy ... let them also who love thy name be joyful.

Matthew 5:12 – Rejoice, and be exceedingly glad...

Romans 14:17 – For the kingdom of God is not meat and drink, but righteousness, and peace, and joy in the Holy Ghost.

Philippians 4:4 – Rejoice in the Lord always; and again I say, Rejoice.

Zukhruf 43:70 – Enter the Garden, you and your wives, to be made glad.

İnsan 76:11 – Therefore, Allah has warded off from them the evil of that day, and has made them find brightness and joy.

* * * *

Note: Verses in the Qur'an which speak about having joy refer primarily to life in the hereafter.

149

Are there examples in the Holy Books where God gives physical healing to people?

^{Bible} **Yes / No** ^{Qur'an}

Exodus 15:26 – I am the LORD that healeth thee.

Psalm 103:2-3 – (2) Bless the LORD, O my soul, and forget not all his benefits: (3) who forgiveth all thine iniquities, who healeth all thy diseases.

Matthew 4:23 – And Jesus went about all Galilee, teaching in their synagogues, and preaching the gospel of the kingdom, and healing all manner of sickness and all manner of disease.

Matthew 14:36 – and besought him that they might only touch the hem of his garment; and as many as touched were made perfectly whole.

Acts 5:15-16 – (15) That they brought forth the sick into the streets, and laid them on beds and couches ... (16) and they were healed every one.

1 Corinthians 12:28, 30 – (28) Then the gifts of healing ... (30) Have all the gifts of healing?

* * * *

Note: There are 26 recorded healings by Jesus alone in the New Testament, but there are no examples of God giving any physical healing to people in the Qur'an during Muhammad's lifetime.

150

Are there verses where God encourages believers to use music, dance and singing in their worship?

^{Bible} **Yes** / **No** ^{Qur'an}

Deuteronomy 31:19 – Write ye this song for you, and teach it to the children of Israel; put it in their mouths, that this song may be a witness for me.

Psalm 100:1-2 – (1) Make a joyful noise unto the LORD ... (2) Come before his presence with singing.

Psalm 149:1-6 – (1) Praise ye the LORD... (3) Let them praise his name in the dance: let them sing praises unto him with the timbrel and harp.

Ephesians 5:18-19 – (18) Be filled with the Spirit, (19) Speaking to yourselves in psalms and hymns and spiritual songs, singing and making melody in your heart to the Lord.

Colossians 3:16 – Teaching and admonishing one another, in psalms and hymns and spiritual songs singing with grace in your hearts to the Lord.

James 5:13 – Is any merry? Let him sing psalms.

* * * *

Note: In the Bible there are over 450 verses encouraging music, dance and singing, but there are none like this at all in the Qur'an.

151

According to the manifest purpose of God, is it right for a man to have more than one wife at the same time?

^{Bible} **No** / **Yes** ^{Qur'an}

Genesis 2:23-24 – (23) She shall be called Woman, because she was taken out of Man. (24) Therefore shall a man leave his father and mother and shall cleave unto his wife; and they shall be one flesh.

Deuteronomy 17:17 – Neither shall he multiply wives to himself, that his heart turn not away.

1 Corinthians 7:2 – Let every man have his own wife, and let every woman have her own husband.

1 Timothy 3:2, 12 – (2) A bishop must be blameless, the husband of one wife... (12) Let the deacons be the husbands of one wife...

Nisa 4:3, 24 – (3) And if you feel that you will not deal fairly with the orphans, marry women of your choice, two or three or four. (24) And all married women are forbidden to you except those your right hand possess.

Ahzab 33:21, 32-33, 38, 50 – (21) Verily in the messenger of Allah you have a good example. (32) O you wives of the Prophet! (38) There is no reproach for the Prophet in what Allah has made his due. (50) A believing woman if she gives herself unto the Prophet and the Prophet desire to ask her in marriage, a privilege for you only, not for the rest of believers.

152

Could a man possibly deal equally with his wives if he had more than one wife at the same time?

^{Bible} <u>**No**</u> / <u>**No**</u> ^{Qur'an}

Genesis 21:9-11 – (9) And Sarah saw the son of Hagar, the Egyptian, whom she had born unto Abraham, mocking. (10) Wherefore she said unto Abraham, Cast out this bondwoman and her son; for the son of this bondwoman shall not be heir with my son, even with Isaac. (11) And the thing was very grievous in Abraham's sight because of his son.

Deuteronomy 21:15 – If a man have two wives, one beloved and another hated.

Nehemiah 13:26-27 – (26) Did not Solomon, king of İsrael, sin by these things ... even him did outlandish women cause to sin.

1 Timothy 3:1-4 – (2) A bishop must be blameless, the husband of one wife, vigilant, sober... (4) One that ruleth well his own house...

Nisa 4:3 – And if you fear that you will not deal fairly with the orphans, marry women of your choice, two or three or four; but if you fear that you cannot deal justly (with so many), then only one, or (the captives) that your right hands possess. Thus it is more likely that you will not do injustice.

Nisa 4:129 – You will never be able to deal equally between your wives, however much you may desire to do so.

153

Is a temporary or interim marriage allowable? (Mut'ah / Law of Desire)

^{Bible} **No / Yes** ^{Qur'an}

Malachi 2:16 – For the LORD, the God of Israel, saith that he hateth putting away ... therefore, take heed to your spirit.

1 Corinthians 7:10-13 – (10) And unto the married I command, yet not I, but the Lord, Let not the wife depart from her husband. (11) ... let not the husband put away his wife ... (13) Let her not leave him.

Nisa 4:24 – Lawful to you are all beyond those mentioned, so that you seek them with your wealth in honest wedlock, not in fornication. And those of whom you seek content (by marrying them), give to them their portions as a duty. And there is no sin for you in what you do by mutual agreement after the duty (has been done).

Maide 5:87 – O you who believe! Forbid not the good things which Allah has made lawful for you.

Ahzab 33:28, 49 – (28) Oh Prophet! Say unto your wives: "If you desire the world's life and its adornment, come! I will content you and will release you with a fair release... (49) If you marry believing women and divorce them... release them handsomely.

Talak 65:1 – O Prophet! If you (believers) divorce your wives, divorce them at the end of their waiting period...

154

In the Holy Books are wives viewed as being a sex object, a commodity or a possession of their husbands?

^{Bible} **No** / **Yes** ^{Qur'an}

1 Peter 3:7 – Likewise, ye husbands dwell with them according to knowledge, giving honor unto the wife, as unto the weaker vessel, and as being heirs together of the grace of life, that your prayers be not hindered.

Ephesians 5:22-25 – (22) Wives, submit yourselves unto your own husbands, as unto the Lord. (23) For the husband is the head of the wife, even as Christ is the head of the church: and he is the savior of the body. (24) Therefore as the church is subject unto Christ, so let the wives be to their own husbands in every thing. (25) Husbands, love your wives, even as Christ also loved the church, and gave himself for it.

Baqara 2:223 – Your wives are a tilth (field to be plowed) unto you. Go, then, into your tilth as you will.

Al-i Imran 3:14 – Fair in the eyes of men is the love of things they covet: women and sons, heaped-up hordes of gold and silver; branded horses, cattle and plantations.

155

Is it permissible for a man to buy or capture slave girls and have sex with them?

^{Bible} **No** / **Yes** ^{Qur'an}

1 Corinthians 7:23 – Ye are bought with a price; be not ye the servants of men.

1 Thessalonians 4:3-7 – (3) For this is the will of God, even your sanctification, that ye should abstain from fornication: (4) That every one of you should know how to possess his vessel in sanctification and honour; (5) Not in the lust of concupiscence, even as the Gentiles which know not God.

Nisa 4:24 – And all married women are forbidden to you except those your right hand possess.

Mü'minun 23:5-6 – (5) And those who guard their chastity (their hidden parts), (6) Except for their wives, and what their right hands possess (slaves), for then they are not blamed.

Ma'arij 70:22, 29-30 – (22) Worshippers ... (29) who restrain their carnal desire, (30) save for their wives and slave-girls, for thus they are not blameworthy.

* * * *

Note: Muhammad waged war against towns, took captives and made slaves out of them (Ibni Hişam, vol. 3, p. 335). Suras 4:3 and 33:50 also permit male slave owners to have sex with their slave-girls.

156

Are women required to wear a veil outside the home?

^{Bible} **No** / **Yes** ^{Qur'an}

1 Corinthians 11:15 – But if a woman have long hair, it is a glory to her; for her hair is given her for a covering.

Galatians 5:1, 4 – (1) Stand fast, therefore, in the liberty wherewith Christ hath made us free, and be not entangled again with the yoke of bondage… (4) Christ is become of no effect unto you, whosoever of you are justified by the law; ye are fallen from grace.

Colossians 2:20 – Why… are ye subject to ordinances…?

Nur 24:30-31 – (30) And say to the believing women that they should … (31) draw their veils over their bosoms and display not their ornaments except to their husbands.

Ahzab 33:59 – O Prophet! Tell your wives and your daughters and the women of the believers to draw their cloaks round them (when they go abroad). That will be better, that so they may be recognized and not annoyed.

157

Are women's rights equal to men's?

^{Bible} **<u>Yes</u> / <u>No</u>** ^{Qur'an}

Deuteronomy 16:19 – Thou shalt not respect persons.

2 Chronicles 19:7 – There is no iniquity with the LORD our God, nor respect of persons.

Acts 15:8-9 – (8) God, which knoweth the hearts... (9) put no difference between us and them.

Romans 2:11 – There is no respect of persons with God.

Galatians 2:6 – God accepteth no man's person.

Galatians 3:28 – There is neither Jew nor Greek, there is neither bond nor free, there is neither male nor female: for ye are all one in Christ.

James 2:9 – But if ye have respect to persons, ye commit sin, and are ... transgressors.

Bakara 2:228, 282 – (228) And women have rights similar to those of men ... and men are a degree above them. (282) Call in two witnesses from among your men, and if two men are not at hand, then one man and two women of such.

Nisa 4:3, 11, 34, 176 – (3) marry women of your choice, two or three or four... (11) Allah thus commands you concerning the division for your children: to the male, a portion equal to that of two females... (34) Men are the protectors of women because they have more strength.

158

Is it ever permissible for a man to beat his wife?

^{Bible} **No / <u>Yes</u>** ^{Qur'an}

Ephesians 5:25-29 – (25) Husbands, love your wives, even as Christ also loved the church, and gave himself for it, That he might sanctify and cleanse it with the washing of water by the word... (28) So ought men to love their wives as their own bodies. He that loveth his wife loveth himself. (29) For no man ever yet hated his own flesh, but nourisheth and cherisheth it, even as the Lord the church.

Colossians 3:19 – Husbands love your wives and be not bitter against them.

1 Peter 3:7 – Ye husbands, dwell with them according to knowledge, giving honour unto the wife, as unto the weaker vessel, and as being heirs together of the grace of life, that your prayers be not hindered.

Bakara 2:36 – But Satan caused them to swerve from it (the garden), and expelled them from their former state. "Go down" We said, "your offspring enemies to each other.

Nisa 4:34 – As for those from whom you fear disloyalty, admonish them and banish them to beds apart, and beat them (lightly, without visible injury). Then if they obey you, seek not a way against them. For Allah is High, Sublime.

159

Is it permissible for a Christian or a Muslim to marry people of a different faith?

^{Bible} **No / Yes** ^{Qur'an}

Deuteronomy 7:3 – Neither shalt thou make marriages with them.

Nehemiah 13:26-27 – (26)Did not Solomon, King of İsrael, sin by... (27)marrying strange wives?

1 Corinthians 7:28, 39 – (28) If a virgin marry, she hath not sinned ... (39) She is at liberty to be married to whom she will, only in the Lord.

2 Corinthians 6:14, 17 – (14) Be ye not unequally yoked together with unbelievers; for what fellowship hath righteousness with unrighteousness? And what communion hath light with darkness? ... (17) Wherefore come out from among them, and be ye separate, saith the Lord.

Maide 5:5 – This day are (all) good things made lawful for you... And so are the virtuous women of the believers, and the virtuous women of those who received the Scripture before you lawful for you when you give them their marriage portions and live with them in honour, not in fornication, nor taking them as secret concubines.

160

If a person gets a divorce from their spouse for a reason other than adultery, are they allowed to remarry?

^{Bible} **No / Yes** ^{Qur'an}

Matthew 5:32 – Whosoever shall put away his wife, saving for the cause of fornication, causeth her to commit adultery; and whosoever shall marry her that is divorced committeth adultery.

Matthew 19:3-9 – (3) The Pharisees also came unto Him, tempting Him, and saying unto Him, "Is it lawful for a man to put away his wife for every cause?" (4) And He answered and said unto them, "Have ye not read that He which made them at the beginning 'made them male and female,' (5) and said, 'For this cause shall a man leave father and mother and shall cleave to his wife, and they twain shall be one flesh'? (6) Wherefore they are no more twain, but one flesh. What therefore God hath joined together, let not man put asunder..." (9) And I say unto you, whoever shall put away his wife, except it be for fornication, and shall marry another, committeth adultery; and whoso marrieth her which is put away doth commit adultery."

Bakara 2:231-232 – (231) When you have divorced your wives... let them go in kindness. (232) When you divorce women... do not prevent them from remarrying...

Tahrim 66:5 – It may happen that his Lord, if he divorces you, will give him in your place better wives than yourselves ... both formerly married and virgins.

161

Is it the object of a Christian to act like Christ and the object of a Muslim to act like Muhammad?

^{Bible} **Yes / Yes** ^{Qur'an}

Matthew 10:24-25 – (25) It is enough for the disciple that he be like his master.

Luke 6:40 – The disciple is not above his master: but every one that is perfect shall be as his master.

John 10:27-28 – (27) My sheep hear my voice, and I know them and they follow me. (28) And I give unto them eternal life; and they shall never perish.

John 14:15, 23-24 – (15) If ye love me, keep my commandments. (23) Jesus answered ... If a man love me, he will keep my words: and my Father will love him ... (24) He that loveth me not keepeth not my sayings.

Al-i İmran 3:31 – Say: If ye do love Allah, Follow me: Allah will love you and forgive your sins.

Al-i İmran 3:55 – Allah said: "O Jesus! I am... setting those who follow you above those who disbelieve until the Day of Resurrection...

Nisa 4:80 – Whoever obeys the Messenger obeys Allah ...

Ahzab 33:21 – Verily in the messenger of Allah you have a good example.

Zukhruf 43:63 – Jesus ... fear Allah and obey me.

Enemies and Warfare

162

In the Holy Books is there a prominent theme that one particular faith should have the goal to forcefully dominate all other religions?

^{Bible} **No** / **Yes** ^{Qur'an}

Luke 17:20-21 – (20) The kingdom of God cometh not with observation: (21) Neither shall they say, Lo here! or, lo there! for, behold, the kingdom of God is within you.

Romans 14:17, 22 – (17) For the kingdom of God is not meat and drink; but righteousness, and peace, and joy in the Holy Ghost. (22) Hast thou faith? Have it unto thyself before God.

Al-i İmran 3:19-20 – (19) The (true) religion in the sight of Allah is Islam. Those who formerly received the Scripture disagreed among themselves through jealousy only after knowledge came to them... (20) If they become Muslims they shall be rightly guided.

Tevbe 9:33 – It is He who has sent His messenger with the guidance and the religion of truth to make it triumphant above all religion.

Saf 61:8-9 – (8) Allah will perfect his light, much as the disbelievers may dislike it. (9) He it is who has sent His messenger with guidance and the Religion of Truth, so that He may exalt it above all religions.

163

In religious affairs, should the use of force and compulsion ever be sanctioned?

^{Bible} **No** / **No** ^{Qur'an}

2 Timothy 2:24-25 – (24) And the servant of the Lord must not strive, but be gentle unto all men, apt to teach, patient, (25) In meekness instructing those that oppose themselves.

Philemon 14 – But without thy mind would I do nothing, that thy benefit should not be, as it were of necessity but willingly.

1 Peter 5:2 – Feed the flock of God which is among you, taking the oversight thereof, not by constraint, but willingly; not for filthy lucre, but of a ready mind.

Bakara 2:256 – There is no compulsion in religion.

Al-i İmran 3:20 – If they become Muslims, they shall be rightly guided; if they turn away, then your duty is only to inform them.

Nisa 4:90 – So, if they keep away from you and wage not war against you and offer you peace, Allah allows you no way against them.

Hud 11:28 – Shall we compel you to accept it while you dislike it?

Kehf 18:29 – Now whosoever will, may believe, and whosoever will, may disbelieve.

Kaf 50:45 – You O Muhammad are in no wise a compeller over them. But warn by the Qur'an.

164

Does God encourage believers today to fight and war against people of different beliefs till their own religion triumphs? (Holy War / Jihad)

^{Bible} **No / Yes** ^{Qur'an}

Romans 12:17-19 – (17) Recompense no man evil for evil ... (18) If it be possible, as much as lieth in you, live peaceably with all men. (19) Beloved, avenge not yourselves, but rather give place unto wrath ... Vengeance is mine; I will repay, saith the Lord.

Hebrews 12:14 – Follow peace with all men, and holiness, without which no man shall see the Lord.

James 1:20 – For the wrath of man worketh not the righteousness of God.

Bakara 2:190-193 – (190) Fight for the sake of Allah ... (191) Kill them wherever you find them ... for tumult and persecution are worse than killing ... (193) And fight them until ... religion is for Allah.

Tevbe 9:29 – Fight against those from among the People of the Scripture who do not believe in Allah.

* * * *

Note: Jihad is one the largest subjects in the Qur'an: 139 verses out of 6,236 = 1 out of every 45 verses. The Hadith is 21% about Jihad: The Sirah (the biography of Muhammad) is 67% about Jihad. 64% of the Qur'an is malevolent against the "Kafir".

165

If a person becomes an apostate from their own mother religion or decides to change their religion, should they be killed?

Bible **No / Yes** Qur'an

1 Timothy 4:1 – Now the Spirit speaketh expressly, that in the latter times some shall depart from the faith, giving heed to seducing spirits, and doctrines of devils.

Hebrews 3:12-13 – (12) Take heed, brethren, lest there be in any of you an evil heart of unbelief, in departing from the living God. (13) But exhort one another daily, while it is called Today, lest any of you be hardened through the deceitfulness of sin.

Nisa 4:89 – And if they turn back (to enmity) then seize them and slay them wherever you find them, and choose no friend or helper from among them.

* * * *

Note: The following quotation of Muhammad about apostates from the Hadith: Allah's Apostle, "Whoever changed his Islamic religion, then kill him." (Sahih Bukhari: Vol. 9, Book 84, no. 57-58, cf. Vol. 4) "They will abandon Islam as an arrow going through game. Their belief will not go beyond their throats (i.e. they will have practically no belief), so wherever you meet them, kill them, for he who kills them shall get a reward on the Day of Resurrection." (Sahih Bukhari: Vol 4, Book 56, No. 808)

166

Is fighting against family, friends or even brethren sometimes prescribed?

^{Bible} **No / Yes** ^{Qur'an}

1 Corinthians 7:13-24 – (13) The woman who hath an husband that believeth not, and if he be pleased to dwell with her, let her not leave him. (14) For the unbelieving husband is sanctified by the wife, and the unbelieving wife is sanctified by the husband ... (16) For what knowest thou, O wife, whether thou shalt save thy husband? O man, whether thou shalt save thy wife?

Ephesians 5:25-29 – (25) Husbands love your wives, even as Christ also loved the church, and gave himself for it, (28) So ought men to love their wives as their own bodies. He that loveth his wife loveth himself. (29) For no man ever yet hated his own flesh, but nourisheth and cherish it, even as the Lord the church.

Mujadila 58:22 – You will find no believers in Allah and the Last Day on friendly terms with those who oppose Allah and His messengers, even though they be their fathers, their sons, their brothers, or their kindred... Allah's party will surely triumph.

Taghabun 64:14 – O believers, among your wives and your children there are enemies for you, therefore beware of them.

167

Does God want believers today to kill others of a different faith even if it goes against their own conscience?

^{Bible} **No / <u>Yes</u>** ^{Qur'an}

Acts 24:16 – And herein do I exercise myself, to have always a conscience void of offence toward God, and *toward* men.

1 Timothy 1:5 – Now the end of the commandment is charity out of a pure heart, and of a good conscience, and of faith unfeigned.

1 Timothy 1:19 – Holding faith, and a good conscience...

1 Peter 3:16 – Having a good conscience, that, whereas they speak evil of you, as of evildoers, they may be ashamed that falsely accuse your good conversation in Christ.

Bakara 2:216 – Fighting is obligatory for you though it be disliked by you; but it may be that you hate a thing although it is good for you, and love a thing although it is bad for you. Allah knows, but you know not.

Enfal 8:17 – You (believers) slew them not, but Allah slew them. And you (Muhammad) did not throw when you threw, but Allah threw, that He might test the believers by a fair test from Him.

* * * *

Note: cf. Hadith, Sahih Muslim, 4661-4662, Ch. 789.

168

Is striving and fighting against people of a different faith seen as something that is basically good?

^{Bible} **No** / **Yes** ^{Qur'an}

Galatians 5:19-21 – (19) Now the works of the flesh are manifest, which are these ... (20) hatred, variance, emulations, wrath, strife, seditions ... (21) envyings, murders ... and such like ... they who do such things shall not inherit the kingdom of God.

James 4:1, 8 – (1) From where come wars and fightings among you? Come they not hence, even of your lusts? (8) Cleanse your hands ye sinners; and purify your hearts, ye double minded.

Tebve 9:41 – Go forth, whether light or heavy, and strive with your wealth and your lives in the cause of Allah. That is better for you, if you only knew.

Ankebut 29:6 – And whoever strives only strives for (the benefit of) himself.

Saf 61:11 – O you who have believed ... strive in the cause of Allah with your wealth and your lives. That is better for you if you should know.

* * * *

Note: See the Hadith in Bukhari Vol. 8, No. 3777.

169

Would God have encouraged Muhammad to start multiple wars of aggression to spread Islam?

_{Bible} **No / Yes** _{Qur'an}

John 18:36 – Jesus answered, My kingdom is not of this world; if my kingdom were of this world, then would my servants fight.

2 Corinthians 10:3-5 – (3) We do not war after the flesh (4) (The weapons of our warfare are not carnal.)

---

1. The Battle of **Badr**: (March 624) Al-i İmran 3:13, 123; Anfâl 8:5-19, 41-44.

2. The Battle of **Uhud**: (March 625) Al-i İmran 3:121-122; 3:140, 165-172.

3. The Battle of **Hendek**: (Feburary 627) The Trench. Ahzab 33:9-12, 25-27.

4. The Battle of **Hudeybiye**: (March 628) Fetih 48:1-3, 22-27.

5. The Battle of **Muta**: (August 629) Baqara 2:191-193.

6. The Battle of **Hunayn**: (January 630) Tevbe 9:25-27.

7. The Battle of **Tebük**: (October 630) Tevbe 9:38-40, 42-52, 65-66, 81-83, 86-87, 90, 93, 117.

8. The Battle of **Mekka**: (December 630) Tevbe 9:12; Kasas 28:85; Saf 61:13; Nasr 110:1-3.

170

In the Holy Books, is fighting against people of the Scripture encouraged?

^{Bible} **No / Yes** ^{Qur'an}

Romans 12:18 – If it be possible, as much as lieth in you, live peaceably with all men.

1 Peter 3:14-17 – (14) But if ye suffer for righteousness' sake, happy are ye; and be not afraid of their terror, neither be troubled... (15) But sanctify the Lord God in your hearts, and be ready always to give an answer to every man that asketh you a reason of the hope that is in you, with meekness and fear. (16) Having a good conscience, that, whereas they speak evil of you, as of evildoers, they may be ashamed that falsely accuse your good conversation in Christ. (17) For it is better, if the will of God be so, that ye suffer for well-doing than for evil-doing.

Tevbe 9:29 – Fight against those from among the People of the Scripture who do not believe in Allah nor the Last Day; who do not forbid what Allah and His messenger have forbidden, and who do not adopt the religion of truth until they pay the tribute out of hand, utterly subdued.

Ahzab 33:26 – And He brought down those of the People of the Scripture who supported them down from their strongholds, and cast panic into their hearts. Some you slew, and you made captive others.

171

Is aggressive and offensive warfare and fighting against nonbelievers encouraged in the Holy Books for believers today? (Jihad)

^{Bible} **No / Yes** ^{Qur'an}

Ephesians 6:12 – For we wrestle not against flesh and blood, but against principalities, against powers, against the rulers of the darkness of this world, against spiritual wickedness in high *places.*

1 Timothy 2:1-3 – (1) I exhort therefore, that, first of all, supplications, prayers, intercessions, and giving of thanks, be made for all men; (2) For kings, and for all that are in authority; that we may lead a quiet and peaceable life in all godliness and honesty. (3) For this is good and acceptable in the sight of God our Saviour.

Nisa 4:76-77 – (76) Those who believe fight for the cause of Allah ... (77) but when fighting was prescribed for them, behold! ... "Our Lord! Why have you ordained fighting for us? If only You would give us respite for a while!" Say: ... "The enjoyment of this world is short; and the Hereafter will be better for him who fears Allah."

Tevbe 9:123 – O you who believe, fight those of the unbelievers near you and let them see how harsh you can be. Know that Allah is with the righteous.

172

Would God encourage believers today to pillage and plunder people of a different faith?

^{Bible} **No / Yes** ^{Qur'an}

Genesis 14:23 – I will not take any thing that is thine, lest thou shouldest say, I have made Abram rich.

Exodus 20:15, 17 – (15) Thou shalt not steal ... (17) Thou shalt not covet thy neighbour's house, thou shalt not covet thy neighbour's wife.

2 Corinthians 6:3 – Giving no offence in any thing, that the ministry be not blamed:

Ephesians 4:27-28 – (27) Neither give place to the devil. (28) Let him that stole steal no more but, rather let him labour, working with his hands... that he may have to give to him that needeth.

Enfal 8:1, 41 – (1) They ask you (O Muhammad) about the spoils of war. Say: "The spoils of war belong to Allah and the messenger ... (41) And know that whatever you take as spoils of war, a fifth thereof is for Allah, and for the messenger.

Hashr 59:7 – That which Allah gives as spoil to His messenger from the people of townships, it is for Allah and His messenger...

* * * *

Note: Muhammad made his living by plundering other's goods: (Ibni Hişam, Vol. 2, No. 318 ff.)

173

Does God want believers today to use terror and harshness against their enemies?

<u>Bible</u> **No** / **Yes** ^{Qur'an}

Jeremiah 22:3 – Thus saith the LORD, Execute ye judgment and righteousness, and deliver the spoiled out of the hand of the oppressor; and do no wrong, do no violence ... neither shed innocent blood.

2 Timothy 2:24-25 – (24) And the servant of the Lord must not strive; but be gentle unto all men, apt to teach, patient, (25) In meekness instructing those who oppose themselves.

A'raf 7:4 – How many a township have We destroyed! As a raid by night, or while they were resting at midday, Our terror came to them.

Enfal 8:12 – I will throw fear into the hearts of those who disbelieve. Then smite the necks and smite of them each finger.

Enfal 8:57 – If you come on them in the war, deal with them so as to strike fear in those who are behind them...

Enfal 8:67 – It is not for any prophet to have captives until he has made slaughter in the land.

Tevbe 9:73, 123 – (73) O prophet! Strive against the disbelievers and hypocrites. Be harsh with them... (123) O you who believe! Fight the disbelievers who are near you, and let them find a harshness in you.

174

Would God want believers today to carry out the law of retribution? (an eye for an eye, and a tooth for a tooth / Kısas)

Bible **No** / **Yes** Qur'an

Matthew 5:39 – But I say unto you that ye resist not evil, but whosoever shall smite thee on thy right cheek, turn to him the other also.

Romans 12:19-21 – (19) Dearly beloved, avenge not yourselves, but *rather* give place unto wrath: for it is written, Vengeance *is* mine; I will repay, saith the Lord. (20) If thine enemy hunger, feed him; if he thirst, give him drink ... (21) Be not overcome of evil, but overcome evil with good.

Hebrews 10:30 – For we know him that hath said, Vengeance belongeth unto me, I will recompense, saith the Lord... The Lord shall judge his people.

Bakara 2:194 – If anyone attacks you, attack him with the like of that with which he attacked you.

Nahl 16:126 – If you punish, then punish with the like of that wherewith you were afflicted...

Shura 42:40-41 – (40) The recompense of an ill-deed is an ill-deed like thereof ... (41) Those who avenge themselves after they have been wronged, cannot be held blameworthy.

175

Would a holy God encourage believers to take revenge into their own hands?

^{Bible} **No** / **Yes** ^{Qur'an}

Deuteronomy 32:35-36 – (35) To me belongeth vengeance, and recompence ... (36) For the LORD shall judge his people.

Romans 2:1 – Therefore, thou are inexcusable, O man, whosoever thou art that judgest; for wherein thou judgest another, thou condemnest thyself.

Romans 12:14-18 – (14) Bless them which persecute you; bless, and curse not... (17) Recompense to no man evil for evil... (18) If it be possible, as much as lieth in you, live peaceably with all men. (19) Dearly beloved, avenge not yourselves, but rather give place unto wrath; for it is written, "Vengeance is Mine, I will repay," saith the Lord.

Bakara 2:178, 179 – (178) O you who believe! The law of retribution is prescribed for you in the matter of the murdered... (179) In this law of retribution there is life for you, O people of understanding, that perhaps you shall be Godfearing.

Maide 5:45 – And We ordained for them therein: The life for the life, and the eye for the eye, and the nose for the nose, and the ear for the ear, and the tooth for the tooth, and for wounds retaliation.

176

Would a holy God encourage believers to curse their enemies?

^{Bible} **No** / **Yes** ^{Qur'an}

Luke 6:27-28 – (27) But I say unto you which hear, Love your enemies, do good to them which hate you, (28) Bless them that curse you, and pray for them which despitefully use you.

Luke 23:33-34 – (33) And when they were come to the place which is called Calvary, there they crucified him… (34) Then said Jesus, Father, forgive them; for they know not what they do.

James 3:9-10 – (9) Therewith bless we God, even the Father; and therewith curse we men, which are made after the similitude of God. (10) Out of the same mouth proceedeth blessing and cursing. My brethren, these things ought not so to be.

Bakara 2:159 – Those that hide the clear proofs and guidance We have revealed, after We have proclaimed them in the Scriptures, shall be cursed by Allah, and by those who have the power to curse.

Al-i İmran 3:61 – And those who dispute with you concerning him (Jesus), after the knowledge which has come to you, say (to them): "Come! Let us summon our sons and your sons, and our women and your women, and ourselves and yourselves, then we will pray humbly and invoke the curse of Allah upon those who lie."

177

Does God consider the Jews to be under a curse or damned as a nation?

_{Bible} **No** / <u>Yes</u> _{Qur'an}

Genesis 12:1-3 – (1) Now the LORD had said unto Abram... (2) And I will make of thee a great nation, and I will bless thee, and make thy name great; and thou shalt be a blessing: (3) And I will bless them that bless thee, and curse him that curseth thee: and in thee shall all families of the earth be blessed.

Jeremiah 31:37 – If heaven above can be measured ... I will also cast off all the seed of Israel for all they have done, saith the Lord.

Romans 11:1-2 – (1) I say then, Hath God cast away his people? God forbid ... (2) God hath not cast away his people which he foreknew.

Romans 12:14 – Bless them... and curse not.

Bakara 2:88-89 – (88) They (the Jews) ... Allah has cursed them for their unbelief ... (89) May Allah's curse be on the disbelievers.

Maide 5:12-13 – (12) Allah made a covenant of old with the Children of Israel ... (13) And because of their breaking their covenant, We have cursed them and made hard their hearts.

* * * *

Note: The Medina portion of the Qur'an is 11% anti-Jewish. Hitler's *Mein Kampf* was only 7% anti-Jewish.

178

Are those who fight considered better than those who don't fight?

^{Bible} **No / Yes** ^{Qur'an}

1 Samuel 30:23-24 – (23) Then said David ... with that which the LORD hath given us, who hath preserved us, and delivered the company that came against us into our hand. (24) ... as his part is that goeth down to the battle, so shall his part be that tarrieth by the stuff; they shall part alike.

Nisa 4:77 – "Our Lord! Why have you ordained fighting for us?... Say (to them, O Muhammad): "The enjoyment of this world is short; and the Hereafter will be better for him who fears Allah.

Nisa 4:95 – Those of the believers who sit (at home in Medina), other than those who have a (disabling) hurt, are not equal with those who strive for the cause of Allah with their wealth and their lives. Allah has conferred on those who strive with their wealth and their lives a rank above the ones who sit (at home).

Tevbe 9:19-20 – (19) Have you made the (mere obligation of) giving water to the pilgrims and the maintenance of the Inviolable Mosque as (equal to the works of) those who have believed in Allah and the Last Day and fought for His cause? They are not equal in the sight of Allah. He does not guide the wrongdoers. (20) Those who believe and have left their homes and fought for Allah's cause with their wealth and their lives are of much greater worth in Allah's sight. They are the triumphant.

179

Do the Holy Books encourage warfare by stating that punishment in hell is promised to noncombatants and by giving a guarantee of entrance into heaven as a reward for those who fight and die in the cause of God or Allah? (Jihad)

^{Bible} **No / Yes** ^{Qur'an}

Romans 12:17-21 – (17) Recompense to no man evil for evil... (18) If it be possible, as much as lieth in you, live peaceably with all men. (19) Dearly beloved, avenge not yourselves... (21) Be not overcome by evil, but overcome evil with good.

James 1:20 – For the wrath of man worketh not the righteousness of God.

James 2:11 – Do not kill... yet if thou kill, thou art become a transgressor of the law...

James 4:1, 8 – (1) From whence come wars and fightings among you? Come they not hence...

Nisa 4:77 – "Our Lord! Why have you ordained fighting for us? ... Say (to them, O Muhammad): the Hereafter will be better for him who fears Allah.

Fath 48:16 – Tell the desert Arabs who were left behind: "You will soon be called upon to fight a mighty people. You will have to fight them, or they will submit ... if you turn your backs as you did before, Allah will punish you with a painful torment.

Historical Events

180

After creating the world, did God rest on the seventh day to leave an important example for mankind to follow? (Sabbath or Shabbat)

_{Bible} **Yes** / **No** _{Qur'an}

Exodus 20:8-10 – (8) Remember the sabbath day, to keep it holy. (9) Six days shalt thou labour and do all thy work; (10) But the seventh day is the sabbath of the LORD thy God; in it thou shalt not do any work, thou, nor thy son, nor thy daughter, thy manservant.

Exodus 31:13-17 – (13) Verily my Sabbaths ye shall keep... (14) Ye shall keep the sabbath therefore; for it is holy unto you... (15) Six days may work be done; but in the seventh is the sabbath of rest, holy to the LORD... (16) the children of Israel shall keep the Sabbath, to observe the sabbath throughout their generations, for a perpetual covenant. (17) It is a sign between me and the children of Israel forever; for in six days the LORD made heaven and earth, and on the seventh day he rested, and was refreshed.

Hebrews 4:4, 9-10 – (4) For he spoke in a certain place of the seventh day in this wise, And God did rest the seventh day from all his works. (9) There remaineth, therefore, a rest to the people of God.

Kaf 50:38 – And verily We created the heavens and the earth, and all that is between them, in six days, and never were We touched by fatigue.

181

Did God create people in His own image and likeness?

^{Bible} **Yes** / **No** ^{Qur'an}

Genesis 1:26-28 – (26) And God said, Let us make man in our image, after our likeness: and let them have dominion over the fish of the sea, and over the fowl of the air, and over the cattle, and over all the earth, and over every creeping thing that creepeth upon the earth. (27) So God created man in his own image, in the image of God created he him; male and female created he them. (28) And God blessed them, and God said unto them, Be fruitful, and multiply, and replenish the earth, and subdue it: and have dominion over the fish of the sea, and over the fowl of the air, and over every living thing that moveth upon the earth.

1 Corinthians 11:7 – For a man indeed ought not to cover his head, forasmuch as he is the image and glory of God: But the woman is the glory of the man.

Nisa 4:28 – For man was created weak.

İbrahim 14:34 – Surely man is a wrong-doer, ungrateful!

Shura 42:11 – The Creator ... he made you pairs from your own kind ... There is nothing like him (in the universe, nothing can be compared with him).

Asr 103:2 – Surely man is in a state of loss.

182

When God expelled Adam and Eve from the garden of Eden, did He pronounce that there would be enmity between the man and the woman?

^{Bible} **No / Yes** ^{Qur'an}

Genesis 3:13-15 – (13) And the LORD God said unto the woman, What is this that thou hast done? And the woman said, The serpent beguiled me, and I did eat. (14) And the LORD God said unto the serpent, Because thou hast done this, thou art cursed above all cattle, and above every beast of the field; upon thy belly shalt thou go, and dust shalt thou eat all the days of thy life: (15) And I will put enmity between thee and the woman, and between thy seed and her seed...

A'raf 7:23-25 – (23) They said, "Our Lord! We have wronged ourselves. If you forgive us not and have not mercy on us, we are of the lost!" (24) He said "God down (from hence), one of you a foe to the other. There will be for you on earth a habitation for awhile." (25) He (Allah) said: "There you shall live, and there you shall die, and thence shall you be brought forth."

Taha 20:123 – He said: "Go down, both of you, from the Garden, with enmity one to another.

* * * *

Note: In the Bible the enmity which God pronounced was not between Adam and Eve but between Satan and mankind.

183

In the story of the flood, after one of Noah's sons drowned, did Noah's ark come to rest upon Mt. Judi?

_{Bible} **No** / **Yes** _{Qur'an}

Genesis 6:9-22 – (18) But I will establish My covenant with you; and you shall go into the ark--you, your sons, your wife, and your sons' wives with you.

Genesis 7:7 – And Noah went in, and his sons, and his wife, and his sons' wives with him, into the ark, because of the waters of the flood.

Genesis 8:4, 18 – (4) And the ark rested ... upon the mountains of Ararat. (18) Noah went forth, and his sons.

Genesis 10:1 – Now these are the generations of the sons of Noah: Shem, Ham, and Japheth; and unto them were sons born after the flood.

1 Peter 3:20 – In the days of Noah ... few, that is, eight souls were saved by water.

Hud 11:42-44 – (42) So the ark floated with them on waves like mountains, and Noah cried out to his son who stood apart: "O my son! Ride with us, and do not be with the disbelievers!" (43) He replied; "I shall seek refuge in a mountain, which will protect me from the water." ... And the wave came between them, and he was among the drowned ... (44) The Ark came to rest on Al-Judi.

184

Did God say that the promise of blessing upon Abraham's descendants would specifically come through the lineage of Isaac and not Ishmael?

^{Bible} **Yes / No** ^{Qur'an}

Genesis 16:11-12 – (11) And the angel of the LORD said unto her, Behold, thou art with child and shalt bear a son, and shalt call his name Ishmael ... (12) And he will be a wild man; his hand will be against every man, and every man's hand against him.

Genesis 17:18-21 – (18) And Abraham said unto God, O that Ishmael might live before thee! (19) And God said, Sarah thy wife shall bear thee a son indeed; and thou shalt call his name Isaac: and I will establish my covenant with him for an everlasting covenant, and with his seed after him. (21) But my covenant will I establish with Isaac, which Sarah shall bear unto thee at this set time in the next year.

Galatians 3:16 – Now to Abraham and his seed were the promises made. He saith not, And to seeds, as of many; but as of one...

Nisa 4:163 – We sent revelation upon Abraham and upon Ishmael ... and Jesus.

Meryem 19:54 – Ishmael ... he was a messenger (of Allah), a Prophet.

185

Did Abraham ever travel to Mecca to offer a sacrifice at the Ka'ba?

_{Bible} **No / <u>Yes</u>** _{Qur'an}

1. Ur of the Chaldees (Genesis 11:31; Acts 7:2-4)
2. Haran (Gen. 12:1-4; Acts 7:4)
3. Damascus (Gen. 15:2)
4. Shechem (Gen. 12:6, 7)
5. Bethel (Gen. 12:8)
6. Egypt (Gen. 12:9-20)
7. Bethel (Gen. 13:1-9)
8. Hebron (Gen. 13:10-18)
9. Dan (Gen. 14:1-14)
10. Hobah (Gen. 14:15, 16)
11. Salem (Gen. 14:17-21)
12. Hebron (Gen. 15:1-21; 17:1-27; Gen. 16)
13. Gerar (Gen. 20:1-18)
14. Beersheba (Gen. 21:1-34)
15. Moriah (Gen. 22:1-18)
16. Hebron (Gen. 23:1-20)

Al-i İmran 3:95-97 – (95) Abraham... (96) The First Sanctuary ever built for mankind was that at Becca (Mecca), a blessed place, a guidance to the peoples. (97) In it there are plain signs; the place where Abraham stood.

Hajj 22:26 – We appointed for Abraham the site of the House ... purify My House for those who circumambulate (the Ka'ba).

* * * *

Note: The Bible indicates that Abraham never went to Mecca. He died at the age of 175 in Hebron.

186

Was Abraham ready to offer up his only legitimate son İsaac as a sacrifice unto God?

^{Bible} **Yes** / **No** ^{Qur'an}

Genesis 22:2 9-12 – (2) Take now thy son, thine only son Isaac, whom thou lovest, and get thee into the land of Moriah; and offer him there for a burnt offering upon one of the mountains which I will tell thee of… (9) and Abraham built an altar there, and laid the wood in order, and bound Isaac, his son, and laid him on the altar upon the wood. (10) And Abraham stretched forth his hand, and took the knife to slay his son. (11) And the angel of the Lord called out to him out of heaven, and said, Abraham, Abraham: and he said, Here I am. (12) And he said, Lay not thine hand upon the lad, neither do thou anything unto him; for now I know that thou fearest God, seeing thou has not withheld thy son, thine only son from me.

Saffat 37:100-107 – (102) And when (his son) was old enough to walk with him, (Abraham) said: "O my dear son, I have seen in a dream that I must sacrifice you, so look, what think you?" He said, "O my father! Do that which you are commanded … (107) Then We ransomed him with a tremendous sacrifice.

* * * *

Note: In the Qur'an it is not apparent which son Abraham was going to sacrifice.

187

Was Abraham's son Ishmael considered to be a prophet?

^{Bible} **No** / **Yes** ^{Qur'an}

Genesis 16:7-15 – (11) The angel of the LORD said unto her (Hagar), Behold thou art with child and shalt bear a son, and shalt call his name Ishmael ... (12) And he will be a wild man; his hand will be against every man, and every man's hand against him.

Galatians 4:22-31 – (22) For it is written, that Abraham had two sons, the one by a bondmaid, the other by a freewoman. (23) But he who was of the bondwoman was born after the flesh; but he of the freewoman was by promise. (24) Which things are an allegory: for these are the two covenants; the one from the mount Sinai, which gendereth to bondage, which is Hagar. (25) For this Hagar is mount Sinai in Arabia, and answereth to Jerusalem which now is, and is in bondage with her children. (26) But Jerusalem which is above is free, which is the mother of us all... (30) Nevertheless what saith the scripture? Cast out the bondwoman and her son: for the son of the bondwoman shall not be heir with the son of the freewoman.

Nisa 4:163 – We sent revelation upon you, as We sent it upon ... Abraham and Ishmael.

Meryem 19:54 – And make mention in the book (the story) of Ishmael. He was true to what he was promised. And he was a messenger (of Allah), a Prophet.

188

Was it Abraham who was thrown into a fire because he refused to worship idols?

^{Bible} **No** / <u>Yes</u> ^{Qur'an}

Daniel 3:1-30 – (19) Then was Nebuchadnezzar full of fury, and the form of his visage was changed against Shadrach, Meshach, and Abed-nego: therefore he spake, and commanded that they should heat the furnace one seven times more than it was wont to be heated. (20) And he commanded the most mighty men that were in his army to bind Shadrach, Meshach, and Abed-nego, and to cast them into the burning fiery furnace… (27) And the princes, governors, and captains, and the king's counselors, being gathered together, saw these men, upon whose bodies the fire had no power…

Enbiya 21:51-71 – (66) Abraham said: "Do you then worship, besides Allah, those things that cannot profit you in anything at all, nor harm you? …" (68) They said: "Burn him (immediately) and protect your gods, if you are doing anything. (69) We said, "O fire! Be coolness and peace for Abraham!"

* * * *

Note: In the Bible it was not Abraham who was thrown into a fire because he refused to worship idols; this story is in reference to Shadrach, Meshach and Abednego. cf. Ankebut 29:16-24; Saffat 37:83, 97.

189

When Moses asked to see God's glory, did God actually allow Moses to see the backside of God in a humanlike form?

^{Bible} **Yes** / **No** ^{Qur'an}

Exodus 33:11, 18-23 – (11) the LORD spoke unto Moses face to face... (18) And he said, I beseech thee, show me thy glory. (19) And he said, I will make all my goodness pass before thee, and I will proclaim the name of the LORD before thee; and will be gracious to whom I will be gracious, and will show mercy on whom I will show mercy. (20) And he said, Thou canst not see my face: for there shall no man see me, and live. (21) And the LORD said, Behold, there is a place by me, and thou shalt stand upon a rock: (22) And it shall come to pass, while my glory passeth by, that I will put thee in a cleft of the rock, and will cover thee with my hand while I pass by: (23) And I will take away mine hand, and thou shalt see my back parts: but my face shall not be seen.

A'raf 7:143 – And when Moses came to our appointed place, and His Lord had spoken to him, he said: Show me (Yourself), that I may gaze upon you." He said: "You will not see Me, but gaze upon the mountain! If it stands in its place, then you will see Me. And when his Lord revealed (His) glory to the mountain, He sent it crashing down. And when he woke, he said: "Glory to You! I turn to You repentant, and I am first of (true) believers."

190

Did Haman live in the same time period as Moses and Pharaoh?

^{Bible} **No / Yes** ^{Qur'an}

Exodus 2:9-10 – (9) And Pharoah's daughter said unto her, Take this child away, and nurse it for me ... (10) And she called his name Moses; and she said, Because I drew him out of the water.

Esther 1:1-2 – (1) Now it came to pass in the days of Ahasuerus (this is Ahasuerus which reigned over one hundred and twenty-seven provinces, from India even to Ethiopia), (2) in those days when King Ahasuerus sat on the throne of his kingdom...

Mü'min 40:23-24, 36-37 – (23) And verily We sent Moses with Our revelations and a clear warrant (24) To Pharoah, Haman ... (36) And Pharoah said: "O Haman, build for me a tower, that I may reach the ways."

* * * *

Note: Moses and Pharaoh lived around 1450 B.C.; But Haman in the book of Esther lived 1000 years later during the reign of Ahasuerus (King Xerxes) during 486-474 B.C. Muhammad, being an 'ummi' (an illiterate) who lived during the Jahiliyya (The Age of Ignorance before Islam), did not understand the Biblical chronology and he ended up placing all three of these men together in the same story. (See also A'raf 7:157-158, Kasas 28:1-8, 37 and Ankebut 29:39)

191

Did God institute the Passover feast to commemorate the firstborn of Israel being saved as the death angel passed over them during the last of 10 plagues which God sent upon Egypt?

^{Bible} **Yes / No** ^{Qur'an}

Exodus 12:1-24 – (12) For I will pass through the land of Egypt this night, and will smite the first-born in the land of Egypt... 14. And this day shall be unto you for a memorial; and ye shall keep it a feast to the LORD throughout your generations.

Matthew 26:17-19 – (17) Jesus... I will keep the Passover at thy house with my disciples.

Isra 17:101 – And assuredly We gave Moses nine clear signs... then Pharaoh said unto him: "I consider, O Moses, that you are bewitched."

Neml 27:12 – (This will be one) among nine tokens unto Pharaoh and his people... But when Our signs came to them, plain to see, they said, "This is mere magic."

* * * *

Note: The Passover or tenth plague is not mentioned in the Qur'an. There are only 9 plagues of Moses mentioned in the Qur'an. The Bible in Exodus 7:14 to 12:36 describes TEN plagues.

192

When going out to war was it Saul (Talut) who tested his soldiers by how they drank water?

^{Bible} **No** / **Yes** ^{Qur'an}

Judges 7:2-6 – (2) And the Lord said unto Gideon, The people that are with thee are too many for me to give the Midianites into their hands, lest Israel vaunt themselves against me, saying, Mine own hand hath saved me... (5) ...the Lord said unto Gideon, Every one that lappeth of the water with his tongue, as a dog lappeth, him shalt thou set by himself; likewise every one that boweth down upon his knees to drink. (6) And the number of them that lapped, putting their hand to their mouth, were three hundred men...

Bakara 2:247-252 – (247) Their Prophet said to them: "Allah hath appointed Saul as king over you."... (249) When Saul set forth with the armies, he said: "Allah will test you at the stream: if any drinks of its water, he goes not with my army: Only those who taste not of it go with me: A mere sip out of the hand is excused." But they all drank of it, except a few... (252)

* * * *

Note: In the Bible it was not Saul but Gideon who tested his soldiers by how they drank water. Saul lived during the time of David from around 1010 < 971 B.C. but Gideon lived a hundred years before them from around 1162 < 1122 B.C.

193

Was Jesus born in a stable in Bethlehem?

^{Bible} **Yes** / **No** ^{Qur'an}

Micah 5:2 – But thou, Bethlehem ... out of thee shall he come forth unto me that is to be ruler in Israel, whose goings forth have been from of old, from everlasting.

Matthew 2:1-11 – (1) Now when Jesus was born in Bethlehem of Judaea in the days of Herod the king, behold, there came wise men from the east to Jerusalem, (2) Saying, Where is he that is born King of the Jews? for we have seen his star in the east, and are come to worship him. (3) Herod the king... demanded of them where Christ should be born... (5) And they said unto him, In Bethlehem of Judaea: for thus it is written by the prophet.

Luke 2:4-16 – (4) And Joseph also went up from Galilee, out of the city of Nazareth, into Judaea, unto the city of David, which is called Bethlehem... (5) with Mary his espoused wife, being great with child. (6) And so it was, that, while they were there, the days were accomplished that she should be delivered. (7) And she brought forth her firstborn son, and wrapped him in swaddling clothes, and laid him in a manger; because there was no room for them in the inn... (8) shepherds... (16) found Mary, Joseph, and the babe lying in a manger.

Meryem 19:23 – And the pains of childbirth drove her to a trunk of a palm-tree.

194

Did three wise men from the East follow the Messiah's star to Bethlehem where they found the baby Jesus and prostrated themselves before him in worship?

_{Bible} **Yes** / **No** _{Qur'an}

Matthew 2:1-11 – (1) Now when Jesus was born in Bethlehem of Judaea in the days of Herod the king, behold, there came wise men from the east to Jerusalem, (2) Saying, Where is he that is born King of the Jews? for we have seen his star in the east, and are come to worship him. (4) And when Herod had gathered all the chief priests and scribes...together, he demanded of them where Christ should be born. (5) And they said..., In Bethlehem of Judaea: ...it is written by the prophet, (6) And thou Bethlehem, in the land of Juda...for out of thee shall come a Governor, that shall rule my people Israel. (7) Then Herod, enquired of the wise men ...what time the star appeared. (8) And he sent them to Bethlehem...Go and search diligently for the young child; and when ye have found him, bring me word again...(9) ...they departed; and, lo, the star, which they saw in the east, went before them, till it came and stood over where the young child was. (10) ...they rejoiced with exceeding great joy. (11) And when they were come into the house, they saw the young child with Mary his mother, and fell down, and worshipped him:

* * * *

Note: There is no such story recorded in the Qur'an.

195

Do the writers of the Holy Books ever quote Jewish fables as though they were actual historical events?

Bible No / Yes Qur'an

1 Timothy 1:4 – Neither give heed to fables ... which minister questions rather than godly edifying.

1 Timothy 4:7 – refuse profane and old wive's fables.

2 Timothy 4:4 – And they shall turn away their ears from the truth, and shall be turned unto fables.

Titus 1:14 – Not giving heed to Jewish fables and commandments of men that turn from the truth.

2 Peter 1:16 – For we have not followed cunningly devised fables when we made known unto you the power and coming of our Lord Jesus Christ, but were eyewitnesses of his majesty.

Enfal 8:31 – And when our revelations are recited to them, they say ... "This is nothing but fables of the men of old."

* * * *

Note: Further accusations by Christians and Jews of there being fables found in the Qur'an: See: En'am 6:25, Nahl 16:24, Mu'minun 23:83, Furkan 25:4-5, Neml 27:68, Akhaf 46:17, Kalem 68:15, Mutaffifin 83:13: Other examples of fables found in the Qur'an which were taken from Jewish literature: 19:22-26; 19:2-35; 3:33-47; 18:9-27; 17:1; 19:29-33; 3:46; 5:110; 3:49...

196

Did Jesus ever do any recorded miracles as a child?

^{Bible} **No** / **Yes** ^{Qur'an}

Luke 2:40 – And the child grew, and waxed strong in spirit, filled with wisdom; and the grace of God was upon him.

Luke 3:21-23 – (21) It came to pass, that Jesus, also being baptized ... (23) Jesus himself began to be about thirty years of age.

John 2:9-11 – (9) Water that was made wine ... (11) This beginning of miracles did Jesus in Cana of Galilee, and manifested forth his glory.

Al-i İmran 3:45-46 – (45) the Messiah, Jesus, son of Mary... (46) He will speak to mankind in his cradle and in his manhood, and he is of the righteous.

Al-i İmran 3:49 – He will say: "I bring you a sign from your Lord. From clay I will make for you the likeness of a bird; I shall breathe into it and, by Allah's leave, it shall become a living bird."

Maide 5:110 – "O Jesus, son of Mary!... I strengthened you with the holy spirit so that you spoke to mankind in the cradle as in maturity ... and how you did shape of clay as it were the likeness of a bird by my permission, and did blow upon it, and it was a bird by My permission."

197

Did seven men and a dog actually wake up in a cave after sleeping there for 309 years?

^{Bible} **No** / **Yes** ^{Qur'an}

1 Timothy 4:7 – Refuse profane and old wives' fables.

Titus 1:14 – Not giving heed to Jewish fables and commandments of men that turn from the truth.

2 Timothy 4:4 – And they shall turn away their ears from the truth, and shall be turned unto fables.

Kehf 18:9-25 – (9) Do you consider that the Companions of the Cave and the Bearers of the Inscription were a wonder among our signs? ... (25) So they stayed in their Cave three hundred years and (some) add nine (more).

* * * *

Note: There is no such story in the Bible but there are many warnings that believers should not give heed to Jewish fables. Wikipedia: The Seven Sleepers refers to a group of Christian youths who hid inside a cave outside the city of Ephesus around 250 AD, to escape a persecution of Christians being conducted during the reign of the Roman emperor Decius. Having fallen asleep inside the cave, they purportedly awoke approximately 150-200 years later during the reign of Theodosius II. An outline of this tale appears in Gregory of Tours (538-594).

198

Did Solomon actually gather together an army of demons (jinn), humans and birds to do battle?

^{Bible} **No** / **Yes** ^{Qur'an}

1 Timothy 1:4 – Neither give heed to fables... which minister questions rather than godly edifying.

1 Timothy 4:7 – Refuse profane and old wives' fables.

2 Timothy 4:4 – And they shall turn away their ears from the truth, and shall be turned unto fables.

Titus 1:14 – Not giving heed to Jewish fables...

2 Peter 1:16 – For we have not followed cunningly devised fables when we made known unto you the power and coming of our Lord Jesus Christ, but were eyewitnesses of his majesty.

Neml 27:17 – And there were gathered together unto Solomon his armies of the jinn and humankind, and of the birds, and they were set in battle order.

* * * *

Note: There is no such story in the Bible but there are many warnings that believers should not give heed to Jewish fables. The story about King Solomon, the Hooppe Bird, and the Queen of Sheba in Neml 27:15-44 is a Jewish fable taken from the II Targum of Esther 2nd Cent. A.D.

199

Did God actually turn people into apes for breaking the sabbath?

^{Bible} **No / Yes** ^{Qur'an}

1 Timothy 1:4 – Neither give heed to fables ... which minister questions rather than godly edifying.

1 Timothy 4:7 – Refuse profane and old wives' fables.

2 Timothy 4:4 – And they shall turn away their ears from the truth, and shall be turned unto fables.

Titus 1:14 – Not giving heed to Jewish fables...

2 Peter 1:16 – For we have not followed cunningly devised fables when we made known unto you the power and coming of our Lord Jesus Christ, but were eyewitnesses of his majesty.

Bakara 2:65-66 – (65) And you know of those of you who broke the Sabbath, how We said unto them: "You shall be detested apes." (66) We made their fate (changing into the state of detested apes) an example to their own generation and to those who followed them, and a lesson to the God-fearing.

* * * *

Note: There is no such story in the Bible but there are many warnings that believers should not give heed to Jewish fables. Yusuf Ali in his translation, The Meaning of the Holy Qur'an, admits that this is only a fable: p. 34, footnote 79).

200

Did God promise the land of Palestine specifically to the Jews?

^{Bible} **Yes** / **Yes** ^{Qur'an}

Deuteronomy 30:3-5 – (3) the Lord thy God will turn thy captivity, and have compassion on thee, and will return and gather thee from all the nations where the Lord thy God hath scattered thee… (5) And the LORD thy God will bring thee into the land which thy fathers possessed, and thou shalt possess it.

Ezekiel 37:21-25 – (21) Thus saith the Lord God: Behold, I will take the children of Israel from among the heathen, whither they be gone, and will gather them on every side, and bring them into their own land. (22) And I will make them one nation in the land upon the mountains of Israel … (25) And they shall dwell in the land that I have given to Jacob, my servant, wherein your fathers have dwelt; and they shall dwell therein, even they, and their children, and their children's children forever.

Maide 5:20-21 – (20) And (remember) when Moses said to his people: "O my people! Remember Allah's favor to you, how he placed among you Prophets, and He made you kings, and gave you that (which) He gave not to any (other) of (His) creatures. (21) O my people! Go into the holy land which Allah has ordained for you.

İsra 17:104 – And We said thereafter to the Children of Israel: "Dwell in the land (of Canaan)."

Extra Verses

1. Genesis 17:7, 19; Matthew 24:35; John 1:2-3; John 12:48 / Büruj 85:22.
2. Psalm 119:160; 2 Peter 3:15-16 / Bakara 2:4, 53, 87; Al-i Imran 3:119.
3. Bakara 2:47, 122.
4. Acts 4:16.
5. Psalm 89:34; Jeremiah 36:23-28; Revelation 22:18-19.
6. Hijr 15:9; Kehf 18:27; Kaf 50:29; Hashr 59:23.
7. 1 Peter 1:23 / Jinn 72:26-28.
8. Nisa 4:46.
9. Psalm 74:10; Psalm 103:8, 17-18 / Büruj 85:14, 22.
10. Isaiah 14:24, 27 / Bakara 2:29, 255; Buruj 85:14, 22.
11. Psalm 146:5-6 / Al-i Imran 3:94; A'raf 7:196; Hashr 59:23.
12. Romans 3:1-3 / Fussilat 41:27-28.
13. 2 Timothy 2:15 / Bakara 2:4; Al-i Imran 3:79.
14. John 12:48; John 14:15, 21, 23-24;/ Al-i Imran 3:50, 55; Al-i Imran 3:84, 119; Nisa 4:82; Zumar 39:9; Zukhruf 43:61, 63.
15. John 14:15, 21; John 15:10.
16. Isaiah 5:14 / Bakara 2:61; Al-i Imran 3:93-94; Fetih 48:29.

17. Al-i Imran 3:85; Saf 61:9.
18. Al-i Imran 3:19-20; Kafirun 109:1-6.
19. 1 John 4:1-3; / Bakara 2:2; Nisa 4:82.
20. Galatians 1:8; 1 Corinthians 14:37-38 / Bakara 2:2-4; Fussilet 41:43.
21. 2 Thessalonians 3:6, 14; 1 John 1:7.
22. Psalm 119:86, 160; Matthew 5:18; 1 Peter 1:23.
23. Revelation 12:9 / Shura 26:192-197.
24. Mark 2:17 / A'raf 7:184; Tur 52:29; Nejm 53:2-4.
25. Deuteronomy 4:35; Psalm 86:10; Mark 12:29-32.
26. Isaiah 46:9-10.
27. Matthew 28:19; Mark 9:7; Romans 9:5 / Bakara 2:150; Shuara 26:196-197; Neml 27;91; Shura 42:15; Duhan 44:8; Quraish 106:3.
28. Jeremiah 23:6 / Rahman 55:78; Hashr 59:24.
29. Exodus 15:11; Psalm 99:9; Hebrews 12:9-10; 1 Peter 1:15-16.
30. Psalm 68:4-5; 1 John 2:22-23.
31. Philippians 2:8; 1 Peter 5:5.
32. Isaiah 45:21; Luke 1:47; 1 Timothy 1:15.
33. Enbiya 21:35, 73.
34. Matthew 3:16-17 / Maide 5:116.
35. John 14:11 / Maide 5:117-118.
36. John 12:28, 30 / Taha 20:133.

37. Genesis 1:26; Matthew 5:8; John 5:37; Philippians 2:5-11; Revelation 4:1-5; Revelation 21:3; Revelation 22:3-4.
38. John 12:27-30.
39. Exodus 4:22-23; Deuteronomy 14:1-2; Romans 8:14-18 / Zukhruf 43:16.
40. Hosea 3:1; Ephesians 2:4-6 / En'am 6:141; Tevbe 9:108; Shura 42:40; Saf 61:4.
41. Genesis 1:26; / Bakara 2:23, 30; Isra 17:65.
42. Deuteronomy 10:17; Colossians 3:25; James 2:9 / Nisa 4:11.
43. Ezekiel 18:25; Ezekiel 33:11; Luke 14:22; John 3:16; / Isra 17:45-46; Mu'min 40:35.
44. Habakkuk 1:13; Titus 1:2; 1 John 1:5 / Al-i Imran 3:54; Maide 5:41; Sejde 32:17; Ahzab 33:17; Mujadele 58:10.
45. Esther 9:25; Proverbs 16:30; Ephesians 6:11; 2 John 1:7 / Enfal 8:30; Yunus 10:21.
46. Ephesians 5:19-21; / Maide 5:51.
47. 1 Peter 5:8; 2 Peter 3:9 / Nisa 4:155; Maide 5:13, 41; Enam 6:149; A'raf 7:155-156, 179; Ibrahim 14:4; Nahl 16:93.
48. Deuteronomy 7:9-10; Deuteronomy 32:4; Hebrews 10:23; / Ankebut 29:21; Shura 32:49-50; Fetih 48:14.
49. Acts 10:25-26 / Enbiya 21:98; Sebe' 34:40-41; Zukhruf 43:20.
50. 2 Timothy 2:13; Titus 2:1 / Hijr 15:28-34; Taha 20:116.
51. Job 33:4; Isaiah 48:16; Matthew 3:16; 2 Corinthians 3:17.

52. Genesis 2:7; Job 27:3; Luke 1:30-37; John 4:24.

53. Matthew 1:19-23 / Meryem 19:17, 19-24.

54. John 10:35; John 12:48; 2 Timothy 3:16; 2 Peter 1:20-21.

55. 1 Corinthinas 14:37-38.

56. Luke 24:49; Acts 2:1-4, 16-18.

57. 1 Thessalonians 2:8.

58. Acts 3:5-11; Acts 9:33-35; Acts 9:36-41.

59. 1 Corinthians 14:11-2, 26-27.

60.

61. Nisa 4:38; A'raf 7:27.

62. 2 Peter 2:4; Revelation 12:9.

63. Matthew 8:28-32 / Nahl 16:98.

64. Hajj 22:52.

65. Ephesians 6:11-12 / Nahl 16:100.

66. Luke 1:26-35.

67. 1 Peter 1:20 / Bakara 2:87.

68. Luke 2:40, 52; Luke 5:22.

69. Mark 4:35-41; Mark 6:35-44.

70. John 3:36.

71. Matthew 16:16-17, 20 / Nisa 4:157; Maide 5:17, 72, 75.

72. John 8:58; John 17:5, 16, 24.

73. John 1:1-3, 14; John 6:51, 62.

74. Al-i Imran 3:59.

75. Colossians 1:4, 15-22.
76.
77. Luke 3:22; John 10:9; 1 John 2:1-2 / Al-i Imran 3:59.
78. Isaiah 7:14; 1 John 2:22-23; 1 John 5:20 / Zukhruf 43:81; Jinn 72:3.
79. Daniel 3:25.
80. Matthew 8:2-3; Matthew 9:18; Matthew 14:33; Luke 24:52; Revelation 5:12, 14.
81. Acts 5:30-31 / Maide 5:116, 118.
82. Maide 5:17; Maide 5:116, 118.
83. Titus 2:13; 2 Peter 1:1, 11 / Zukhruf 43:57-59.
84. John 6:48, 51; John 17:3 / Saf 61:8-9.
85. Hebrews 7:27; Hebrews 10:12.
86. Psalm 22:1-31.
87. Matthew 17:22-23; Matthew 20:17-19.
88. Acts 13:14-15; 1 Corinthians 2:2; Revelation 1:18; Revelation 5:9.
89. John 5:28-29; Hebrews 9:28.
90. En'am 6:19, 93.
91. Ibrahim 14:4.
92. Isaiah 8:20 / Nisa 4:166.
93. 1 John 2:22-23 / Al-i Imran 3:3-4.
94. John 20:30-31 / Al-i Imran 3:183; Ankebut 29:50.
95. Tekvir 81:22-25.

96. Al-i Imran 3:97; Neml 27:91; Quraish 106:3.
97. Leviticus 18:15; Acts 17:30 / Ahzab 33:37; Mu'min 40:55; Fatih 48:1-2; Abese 80:1-11; Nasr 110:3.
98. Ahzab 33:21; Saf 61:9.
99. Genesis 3:6.
100. Genesis 6:5; Romans 5:12, 19; Romans 7:18; Romans 8:7.
101. Job 9:20; Psalm 14:3; Isaiah 64:6.
102. Luke 1:46-49.
103.
104. Galatians 5:9 / Nisa 4:31.
105. Exodus 20:15; Romans 12:17-21.
106. Psalm 58:3; John 8:44 / Al-i Imran 3:54; Tevbe 9:3; Nahl 16:106.
107. Romans 1:24.
108. Psalm 94:21, 23 / Kehf 18:46; Mumtehine 60:12.
109. Galatians 5:4.
110. John 18:36; 1 John 2:29; 1 John 4:7; 1 John 5:1.
111. James 2:10 / Nejm 53:32.
112. 1 Corinthians 5:7; Hebrews 7:27; Hebrews 10:12 / En'am 6:164.
113. Yunus 10:108.
114. John 1:41; Romans 15:20-21.
115. John 6:48, 51 / Al-i Imran 3:85.
116. Acts 10:44-48; 1 Peter 3:20-21.

117. Acts 15:28-29.
118. Leviticus 19:2; Leviticus 21:7; 2 Timothy 1:9; Hebrews 12:10; 1 Peter 2:5.
119. 2 Corinthians 6:18; 1 John 3:1 / Zuhurf 43:16.
120. Psalm 119:30; Psalm 119:174; John 1:12 / Hadid 57:22.
121. James 2:10 / Kaari'a 101:6-9.
122. Titus 3:5-6; 1 Peter 2:2; 1 John 5:1.
123. Romans 10:9.
124. Revelation 1:1 / Bakara 2:119.
125. Revelation 8:6; Revelation 15:1; Revelation 16:1.
126. Revelation 13:11-18; Revelation 14:9-12; Revelation 19:20.
127. Nahl 16:92; Enbiya 21:47.
128. John 3:16, 36; Romans 6:23.
129. Matthew 18:8; Revelation 14:10-11.
130. Duhan 44:54; Rahman 55:55-56, 70-74.
131. Muhammad 47:15; Vakia 56:17.
132. 2 Corinthians 11:2; Revelation 21:2.
133. Galatians 5:1, 4; Ephesians 2:8-9.
134.
135. 1 Corinthians 10:31 / Bakara 2:173.
136. Matthew 9:15.
137. Bakara 2:183-185.
138. Nisa 4:103; Jumah 62:9.
139. Luke 6:38; 1 John 3:17 / Mujadila 58:12-13.

140. Enbiya 20:130.
141.
142. Psalm 40:6; Hebrews 10:6, 10-18.
143. Maide 5:101; Zukruf 43:45.
144. John 8:31.
145. Psalm 58:3; Jeremiah 17:5; Romans 3:10, 12 / Yunus 10:38, 94.
146. Fetih 48:28; Saf 61:9.
147. Philippians 3:15-16 / Mu'minun 23:52-54.
148. Psalm 32:11; John 15:11; Galatians 5:22; 1 Thessalonians 5:16.
149. Matthew 10:1, 8; James 5:16.
150. Psalm 47:1, 6-7; Psalm 150:4-6.
151.
152. 1 Timothy 5:21.
153. Bakara 2:229-232.
154. Ahzab 33:50.
155. Nisa 4:3; Ahzab 33:50; Talak 65:4.
156.
157. Deuteronomy 10:17 / Talak 65:4.
158. Nur 24:2.
159. 1 Corinthians 16:22; 2 John 1:10-11.
160. Romans 7:2-3.
161. John 10:30 / Al-i Imran 3:114; Al-i Imran 3:132;

A'raf 7:157; Nur 24:2; Fetih 48:29; Talak 65:4; Kalem 68:4.

162. Al-i Imran 3:85; Tevbe 9:29; Zukhruf 43:52; Muhammad 47:4.

163. Tevbe 9:23; Yunus 10:99-100; Gasiye 88:21-22.

164. James 2:11; James 4:2, 8 / Bakara 2:216; Al-i Imran 3:85; Nisa 4:76; Enfal 8:65; Tevbe 9:5, 33, 14, 111, 123; Hajj 22:39.

165. 1 Timothy 4:1 / Tevbe 9:73.

166. Matthew 15:4-8.

167. 1 Timothy 4:2-3 / Tevbe 9:5; Hajj 22:19.

168. Luke 6:27-28; Romans 12:18; 2 Timothy 2:23-26 / Bakara 2:191-192; Nisa 4:91; Tevbe 9:111, 121.

169. Galatians 5:19-21; Ephesians 56:12; James 4:1.

170. Tevbe 9:30.

171. Tevbe 9:29, 73; Muhammad 47:35.

172. Proverbs 16:19; Proverbs 22:22-23; Romans 12:17-18; 2 Corinthians 6:4.

173. Romans 12:17-19; Hebrews 12:14 / Maide 5:33; Enfal 8:60, 65; Fetih 48:29.

174. Hebrews 1:30 / Bakara 2:178-179; Maide 5:45.

175. Romans 2:2-3.

176.

177. Numbers 22:6, 12; Numbers 23:8, 20; Isaiah 54:10, 17; John 4:22 / Maide 5:51; Tevbe 9:28.

178. Tevbe 9:39.

179. Matthew 26:52 / Al-i Imran 3:169-170; Enfal 8:16; Tevbe 9:81, 111; Hajj 22:58.

180. Exodus 23:12.

181. Genesis 9:6; Isaiah 17:67 / Yusuf 12:53, 100; Qiyamah 75:14; Adiyat 100:6.

182. Bakara 2:36.

183.

184. Galatians 4:30-31.

185. Bakara 2:127.

186. Genesis 17:18-21.

187. En'am 6:85-89.

188. Ankebut 29:16-24; Saffat 37:83, 97.

189. En'am 6:103.

190. Esther 3:1 / Kasas 28:1-8, 37; Ankebut 29:39.

191. Exodus 7:14; Exodus 12:36.

192. 1 Samuel 17:47.

193. Meryem 19:25.

194. Micah 5:2.

195.

196. Meryem 19:29-30.

197. 1 Timothy 1:4; 2 Peter 1:16.

198.

199. Maide 5:60; A'raf 7:163-166.

200. A'raf 7:137.

Acts 17:11

These were more noble than those in Thessalonica, in that they received the word with all readiness of mind, and searched the scriptures daily, whether those things were so.

1 Timothy 4:15-16

Meditate upon these things; give thyself wholly to them; that thy profiting may appear to all. Take heed unto thyself, and unto the doctrine; continue in them: for in doing this thou shalt both save thyself, and them that hear thee.

2 Timothy 2:15

Study to shew thyself approved unto God, a workman that needeth not to be ashamed, rightly dividing the word of truth.

Al-i Imran 3:79

Be worshippers of Allah by virtue of your constant study and teaching of the Scripture.

Zumar 39:9

Can those who know and those who do not know ever be equal? But only men of understanding will pay heed.

Zukhruf 43:61

And when Jesus came with clear proofs (of Allah's sovereignty), he said ... "Fear Allah and obey me."

About the Author

Dan Wickwire was born in California in 1951 and grew up in the city of Bakersfield. His military service included three years in the U.S. army, during which he was trained as a medic, a paratrooper, and a Green Beret. He served a tour of duty as a combat medic in Vietnam.

Dan's education includes:
- Bakersfield College, earning an associate's degree in liberal arts.
- Multnomah School of the Bible, studying Bible, Hebrew, and Greek, and earning a bachelor's degree in theology.
- Columbia Graduate School of Bible & Missions, earning a master's degree in Bible.
- Summer Institute of Linguistics (SIL); University of Washington at Seattle; University of Texas at Arlington; and University of Oklahoma at Norman, studying linguistics. Dan earned a master's degree in linguistics at Pacific Western University.
- Ankara University in Ankara, Turkey, completing one year of doctoral studies in Islamics in the Department of Islamic Theology.

Dan is married to Devri and is the father of three sons: Derek Yekta, Andrew Nadir, and Peter Can. He is an ordained minister who served as a church planting missionary in Turkey for twenty-eight years. Dan and Devri currently reside in the Turkish Republic of Northern Cyprus.

Dan's books can be downloaded at:

danwickwire.com

* *100 Questions About the Bible and the Qur'an*, (in Turkish) 144 pages, 1st Ed. 2001, 2nd Ed. 2003; (in English) 1st Ed. 2003, 2nd Ed. 2004.

* *200 Questions About the Bible and the Qur'an*, 120 pages, 2014. Also available in: Albanian, Arabic, Azeri, Chinese, Dutch, English, Farsi, French, German, Kazak, Korean, Norwegian, Polish, Portuguese, Romanian, Russian, Spanish, and Turkish.

* *An Analytical Analysis of the Similarities and Differences Between the Qur'an and the Bible*, (in Turkish) 216 pages, 2007; (in English) 224 pages, 2007.

* *An Outline of Jihad in Islamic History*, 144 pages, 2015.

* *A Theological Sourcebook*, (in English) 240 pages, 1985; (in Turkish) 240 pages, 1987.

* *Has the Bible Been Changed?* (in Turkish) 48 pages, 1st Ed. 1987; 2nd Ed. 1994; 3rd Ed. 2007; 4th Ed. 2014; (in English) 96 pages, 1st Ed: 1987; 2nd Ed. 2007; 3rd Ed. 2011; 108 pages, 4th Ed. 2014.

* *The Reliability of the Scriptures According to Jewish, Christian and Islamic Sources*, (in Turkish only) 420 pages, 1999.

* *The Role of Prayer and Fasting in Binding and Loosing with Special Reference to the Problem of Reaching the Unreached People of the World Today*, unpublished thesis at Columbia, 78 pages, 1983.

* *The Sevmek Thesis: A Grammatical Analysis of the Turkish Verb System: Illustrated by the verb "Sevmek" = "To Love,"* published thesis (in English and Turkish), 170 pages, 1987; 2nd Ed. 1,000 pages, 2012.

* *The Wickwire Compendium of Islam*, 1,000 pages, 2010.

200 Questions about the Bible and the Qur'an may also be downloaded and printed for free at the authors website in many other languages:

Albanian, Arabic, Azeri, Bosnian, Bulgarian, Chinese, Croatian, Dutch, English, Farsi, French, German, Greek, Hindi, Indonesian, Italian, Kazak, Korean, Norwegian, Polish, Portuguese, Punjabi, Romanian, Russian, Spanish, Turkish, Urdu, and are being translated into many other languages.

www.ingramcontent.com/pod-product-compliance
Lightning Source LLC
Chambersburg PA
CBHW070135080526
44586CB00015B/1704